Duels, Gunfights & Shoot-Outs

Wild Tales from the Land of Enchantment

by Don Bullis

Duels, Gunfights & Shoot-Outs

Wild Tales from the Land of Enchantment

by Don Bullis

Published by Rio Grande Books
Los Ranchos. New Mexico

ISBN 10: 1-890689-63-7
ISBN 13: 978-1-890689-63-6

Library of Congress Cataloging-in-Publication

Bullis, Don.
  Duels, gunfights & shoot-outs : wild tales from the Land of Enchantment / Don Bullis.
    p. cm.
  Includes bibliographical references and index.
  ISBN-13: 978-1-890689-63-6 (pbk. : alk. paper)
  ISBN-10: 1-890689-63-7
  1. Frontier and pioneer life--New Mexico. 2. Gunfights--New Mexico. 3. Outlaws--New Mexico--Biography. 4. Violence--New Mexico--History. 5. Firearms--New Mexico--History. 6. New Mexico--History--19th century. 7. New Mexico--History--20th century. 8. New Mexico--Biography. 9. Gunfights--West (U.S.). 10. Outlaws--West (U.S.)--Biography. 11. Violence--West (U.S.)--History. 12. Firearms--West (U.S.)--History. 13. West (U.S.)--History--19th century. 14. West (U.S.)--History--20th century. 15. West (U.S.)--Biography. I. Title. II. Title: Duels, gunfights and shoot-outs.
  F801.B93 2009
  978.9--dc22
                    2009035796

DEDICATION

Dedicated to my wife, Gloria Bullis:
she has made my travels in
New Mexico a treat for a
quarter of a century.

Table of Contents

(Note: all locations are indicated by the counties of which they are a part in modern New Mexico, not the counties that existed when the events described transpired.)

New Mexico

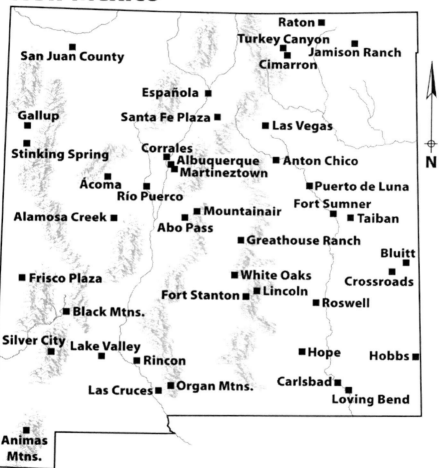

Raton ■
Turkey Canyon
Jamison Ranch ■
Cimarron
San Juan County ■
Española ■
Santa Fe Plaza ■
Las Vegas ■
Gallup
■
Stinking Spring
Corrales
Albuquerque ■ Anton Chico
Martineztown
Ácoma
Puerto de Luna ■
Río Puerco
Fort Sumner ■
Alamosa Creek ■
Mountainair
Taiban ■
Abo Pass
Greathouse Ranch
Bluitt
■
■ Frisco Plaza
White Oaks
Crossroads
Fort Stanton ■ Lincoln
Black Mtns.
Roswell
Silver City
Lake Valley
Hope
Hobbs ■
Rincon
Carlsbad ■
Las Cruces ■ Organ Mtns.
Loving Bend
Animas
Mtns.

N

Introduction

In a Santa Fe saloon, in 1854, two men exchanged words over the merits of a defunct newspaper. The dispute became heated and one of them pulled a pistol and the other a Bowie knife. The man with the knife won and the man with the gun died.

In a Corrales saloon, in 1975, two strangers showed up with intentions of "cleaning out" the place. One of them was armed with a knife, the other with a pistol. The bar's two owners were also armed. When the gunsmoke cleared, the strangers were dead and one of the owners was badly wounded. The other owner died an hour later of a heart attack.

This book includes the details of these two events, and forty-four other violent affairs that occurred across New Mexico during the 121-year interim. Several of the affrays involved lawmen of one kind or another, which is natural enough; lawmen are armed and their work can involve reaction to the use of deadly force. Some duels arose from personal disputes — one as seemingly innocuous as a flock of turkeys — while others were the products of criminal activity. There is no common thread in these tales. Guns were generally the weapons of choice, but a few knives were used. In most cases, someone died as a result of the confrontation, but not always; one Las Cruces gunfight ended with two men wounded, but no one dead.

These events all took place after the Americans arrived in 1846, and for good reason; there is little along these lines to write about during the Spanish and Mexican eras in New Mexico History. From 1598 until 1846, society was largely law-abiding. Communities were small and families extended. The Roman Catholic Church dominated in matters of morality and social standards, and local *padres* and parishes played important parts in community life. The Americans brought changes with them; changes in the criminal justice system; changes in community standards and changes in life-styles. While Spaniards and Mexicans had managed nicely — with a few exceptions — in keeping order in their respective societies, the Americans during Territorial days could not claim as much.

Many of the new arrivals from the east were young men, single, and adventurous. Many of them, especially after the Civil War, came west to begin new lives; but sadly, some of them had much more venal intentions. That is to say, they were thieves of one kind or another. Add to that the fact that many of them went about armed on a daily basis and many of them found recreation and amusement in saloons where a poor grade of hard liquor was the stock in trade. The results were sometimes devastating, as some of the entries in this book amply demonstrate.

Some 19th century wag is reported to have said, "God made men, but Sam Colt made them equal." Maybe not.

Don Bullis
Rio Rancho, New Mexico
October 2009

Abo Pass, Valencia County
1911

Railroad Officer Killed by Thieves
Howe Gang Members Killed in Gunfight With
NM Lawmen & Texas Rangers

A 249-mile railroad line known as the Belen Cut-off between Belen, New Mexico and Texico, on the New Mexico/Texas border, opened in 1907.[1] One unforeseen result of the new line was that it offered thieves an opportunity to rob freight cars as slow-moving trains crawled up the 1¼% grade east-bound on the 25-mile stretch between Belen and the Abo Pass. Often the criminals would board the slow-moving train, enter the cars and throw cargo off to the side of the railroad right-of-way where accomplices in wagons would gather it up. They would also break into and steal from any rail cars left unattended along sidings. This went on for a long time until railroad officials grew weary of the practice, and the accompanying losses.[2]

On Wednesday, January 25, 1911, two railroad officers were sent to investigate the thefts. They boarded an eastbound train at Belen. One of the agents—unnamed in news reports of the day—got off at a flag

Deputy U.S. Marshal Ben Williams (left), U.S. Marshal Creighton Mays Foraker (middle), and W.C. Kennedy (right). Ratón, New Mexico, in July 1894. Photograph courtesy Walter Haussaman, Albuquerque.

stop to send a telegram before they reached the Abo Pass and the train went on without him. Agent J. A. McClure continued on alone. He was never seen alive again.

When McClure failed to return the following day, the chief of the railroad police, Ben Williams (see pages 102-107), took personal charge of the investigation, though due to an injury he could not take part in the actual chase. He immediately suspected homesteader Frank Howe and his two sons, Robert and Guy, who lived near the railroad tracks at Abo. They were leading members of a loosely organized group known as the Abo Pass Gang. Williams also believed that McClure was already dead at that point.

On Friday, January 27, a posse of heavily-armed officers headed by Billy Olds, a railroad special agent and former Arizona Ranger, and Lt. John Collier of the New Mexico Mounted Police[3], reached Abo to hunt for McClure. The search was futile the first day. One rancher reported that he'd heard shots on Wednesday, but feared to investigate and remained indoors the remainder of the day. Other area residents also refused to cooperate with the posse members. Local folks feared the Howes, father and sons.

On the afternoon of the second day, officers found Agent Mc-Clure's body, head down, in a deep well on property belonging to Frank Howe. Close by they also found several large caches of goods stolen from railroad cars, including five wagons laden with corn, dried fruit and chop feed for animals.

Investigation revealed that McClure had been shot from ambush. He had apparently discovered that thieves had stolen corn from a boxcar, and by following a trail of kernels left by a leaking grain bag, he located the outlaw camp. As he neared it, the thieves opened fire, hitting the officer in the wrist, arm and stomach. After he fell, Officer McClure was shot a fourth time, in the top of the head, the bullet exiting at his chin. His body was robbed of all valuables, including a gold watch and a semiautomatic pistol, before it was thrown into the well.

The Howes and four of their horses were gone.

By Sunday, several posses were in pursuit of Howe and his sons, and the Santa Fe Railroad offered a $500 reward for arrest and conviction. Ben Williams believed that the outlaws would head for Mexico, and he was right.

The Howes traveled southeast to Gallinas (later called Holloway), an El Paso & Rock Island Railroad stop south of Corona. They stole a saddle from a rancher along the way. They boarded a southbound freight and rode all the way to Fort Hancock, Texas, about 50 miles south of El Paso, where they were thrown off the train.

When they attempted to cross into Mexico on foot, Tom L. O'Connor, a United States Customs guard, and M. R. Hemly, a Justice of the Peace, attempted to stop them. The outlaws had rifles hidden in the bedrolls they carried, and they opened fire at once. O'Connor fell, mortally wounded with a bullet in the lung. Hemly received a bullet wound to the arm. The Howes then fled east, toward Sierra Blanca, Texas. (Why they did not continue into Mexico is not known.)

At that point, four Texas Rangers from Ysleta joined with the New Mexico lawmen in pursuit of the killers. At about 9:00 p.m. on Tuesday, January 31, the posse overtook the Howes. A gunfight erupted immediately and Robert Howe, the younger of the brothers, was wounded in the leg with the first volley. His older brother and father abandoned him to the posse and fled into a thicket, firing as they ran. Officers surrounded the undergrowth and prepared to stand siege until the morning's light.

In only an hour or so, though, Frank and Guy Howe, father and son, emerged from the brush, rifles in hand and firing as they ran toward the law officers. Officers returned fire and both outlaws fell, shot dead. Ben Williams said later that about 500 shots were fired in the two gun battles with the Howes. Whatever became of Robert is not known except that he was not killed in Texas.

ENDNOTES:

[1] Construction actually began in 1903 but economic hard-times held it up for several years.

[2] It was widely believed that a railroad employee was involved and tipped off

6

the thieves as to which cars contained the most desirable loot. This was not proved, however, and no arrests were ever made.

[3] The New Mexico Mounted Police, the state's first statewide law enforcement organization (1905-21), should not be confused with today's Mounted Police organization, which is made up of civilians who act in support of the New Mexico State Police.

SOURCES:

Albuquerque Morning Journal, January 28, 29, 30, 31, 1911
Randy Dunson, "The Abo Pass Gang"
David F. Myrick, *New Mexico's Railroads*

Acoma Reservation, Valencia County
1952

*State Police Officer Nash P. Garcia Shot,
Killed on Acoma Reservation
Perpetrators in Custody*

Officer Nash Garcia[1] sat in his parked police car along U. S. Route 66 about 20 miles east of Grants on Friday, April 11, 1952. He may have been doing paperwork. A pickup sped past him. Then it turned around and passed him again, operating erratically. The officer took up pursuit.

Garcia followed as the truck turned off the highway about 18 miles east of Grants and drove south on dirt roads across Acoma Pueblo Indian Reservation land for about 19 miles at which point it stopped. As Officer Garcia approached the pickup, two subjects opened fire from ambush with .30-caliber rifles; one from about 100 yards and the other from about 50 feet. They fired nine shots into the police car and Nash Garcia. The officer managed to open the car's door and then fell out onto the ground, severely wounded and unable to return fire. The offenders then beat him about the head with gun-butts to make certain he was dead. They loaded his body into the police car and drove another six miles into reservation land, to a spot near Sandstone Mesa where they abandoned it. They returned the following day, filled the car with brush and set it afire.

Officer Garcia wasn't missed until Sunday morning when he failed to respond to a call from headquarters. State Police Chief Joe Roach said it wasn't unusual for the officer to be out of contact for a day or so, especially if he was working on the reservation. Concern for Garcia's safety

New Mexico State Police Officer Nash P. Garcia

increased when officers contacted his wife and she said she had not heard from him, either. His work, she said, sometimes kept him away from home for several days at a time.

A search and an investigation were initiated. It didn't take long. A local cowboy and several other witnesses told investigators they saw Garcia in pursuit of a pickup truck driven by one of the Felipe brothers: Willie, 31, or Gabriel, 28. On Sunday evening, State Police officers Dick Lewis and Joe Fernandez went to Willie Felipe's house on the Acoma reservation. Felipe offered no resistance and told the officers what he and his brother had done.

"I knew they'd get me," Willie Felipe said later to an Albuquerque *Journal* reporter. "They always get them."

The next morning Willie led a seven-vehicle caravan of officers and other searchers to Sandstone Mesa. They found "...a few pitifully small pieces of charred bone in a pile of ashes on the floor [of the car]."

On Monday evening, April 14, Albuquerque motorcycle policeman Robert Olona, Nash Garcia's cousin, arrested Gabriel Felipe on

North First Street in Albuquerque. Gabriel offered no resistance when taken into custody. He maintained that he took no part in the killing. He asserted that he actually tried to stop Willie from shooting the State Policeman. Officers found Garcia's service revolver in a suitcase in Gabriel Felipe's hotel room along with another gun that belonged to the suspect.

The Felipe brothers were tried, convicted and sentenced to life in federal prison by U. S. District Court Judge Carl Hatch. One of the brothers died in prison and the other was released in the early 1970s.

The motivation for the Felipe brothers' actions has never been positively determined. One report was that they were angry with the officer because he'd previously arrested them for deer poaching. Another source said that Willie and Gabriel felt as though Garcia had been "mean" to them in the past. And a local rumor at the time was that the Felipes thought that Garcia was a witch.

ENDNOTE:

[1] Nash Garcia was the first member of the New Mexico State Police to be murdered in the line of duty. Two officers, Walter Taber in 1937 and Delbert Bugg in 1946, were previously killed in motorcycle accidents. A third State Police officer, William Speight, died as he tried to reach a radio tower near Cloudcroft in February of 1949. The State Police Department was created in 1935 and became a division of the New Mexico Department of Public Safety in 1987.

SOURCES:

Albuquerque Journal, April 14 & 15, 1952

Don Bullis, *New Mexico's Finest: Peace Officers Killed in the Line of Duty, 1846-1999*

The Roadrunner (New Mexico State Police Association, Vol. 3, No. 2, Summer, 1992)

State Police records

Alamosa Creek, Socorro County
1898

Train Robbers Kill Three Officers in One-Sided Battle
Bronco Bill Walters Captured in Arizona
Kid Johnson Killed as Red Pipkin Flees in Hail of Lead

At about a quarter before two on the morning of May 23, 1898, armed men boarded the engine of a passenger and express train at Belen, New Mexico. They forced the engineer to move the train on down the line about two miles, where they separated the express car from the rest of the train. They blasted the door off the safe with dynamite and stole the contents. The railroad at the time placed the loss at $500[1]; an Albuquerque newspaper reported it at about $3,500; later historians say $20,000 to $50,000 was taken. The thieves rode off to the west.

A few hours later, Valencia County Sheriff's Deputies Frank Vigil and Dan Bustamente set out from Belen in pursuit of the robbers. Socorro County Sheriff Holm Bursum and Deputy U. S. Marshal Cipriano Baca set out from Socorro on the same mission, but their horses gave out and they turned back to get fresh mounts and more men. Vigil and Bustamente made camp for the night and rode into the Ala-

Bronco Bill Walters

mo Navajo community early on the morning of May 25. A group of Navajo Indians, only two of whom were armed, joined the effort to capture the thieves. The Indians told the deputies that the outlaws were hiding nearby, and they set out immediately.

The posse arrived at the outlaw camp on Alamosa Creek at about 6:00 a.m. Some of the Navajos were able to get in close enough to lead off the bandit's horses before Vigil, Bustamente and two Navajos surrounded the camp. At a range of about 100 yards, Deputy Vigil called out to the men to surrender and the outlaws seemed to comply, standing with their arms at their sides, their rifles leaning against a tree about 10 feet away. The officers approached. At a range of about 35 yards, the outlaws suddenly grabbed their rifles, ducked behind some cottonwood trees and opened fire. Frank Vigil and Dan Bustamente were scarcely able to return fire before they fell, both mortally wounded. One of the bandits was hit in the neck and while his partner tended to the wound, one of the Navajo possemen, Vicente Guerro, opened fire, wounding the outlaw in the hip and shoulder. The bandit fired at the Navajo with his rifle and Guerro fell dead with a bullet in the head.

The other possemen retreated south to Magdalena where they put out the first word of the gun battle. They later returned and recovered the bodies of the fallen officers, which they took to the mining village of Santa Rita (called Riley by the time it became a ghost town in the early 1930s), east of Alamo on the Río Salado. Vigil and Bustamente were buried there, although Vigil's remains were later removed to Belen. An outlaw may also have been killed in the battle, but no source is certain of that and no one suggests who it might have been.

Valencia County Sheriff Jesus Sánchez lauded the bravery of his men in their effort to arrest the bandits, but he pointed out that they put themselves in considerable jeopardy by not having armed themselves with rifles. All four possemen were armed only with revolvers and their handguns were no match for the "improved" Winchester rifles the outlaws used in the gunfight.

Socorro County Sheriff Holm Bursum

The gang of train robbers was made up of William E. "Bronco Bill" Walters[2], Daniel "Red" Pipkin and William "Kid" Johnson,[3] and one or two others, all of whom had long criminal records. Walters in particular was considered one of the worst New Mexico outlaws and had been ordered to "quit the Territory" in 1897. He obviously didn't stay away for long, if indeed he left at all.

Part of the loot from the robbery was in silver dollars which were too heavy to carry. The coins were buried before the posse caught up with the gang. The remainder, in paper money, was also buried near Alamosa Creek—except for a few thousand dollars they kept for immediate needs—before they limped away from the scene of the fight. They made it to Datil, New Mexico, where they stole horses and rode on west to the small town of Geronimo, northwest of Safford on the Gila River. Walters had cowboyed in the area and friends there provided him with shelter and medical attention.

The outlaws lived there openly and spent money freely. On July 4, 1898 the three of them attended a dance held in a schoolhouse near

13

Geronimo. The story goes that Walters asked several of the women present to dance with him, and they all refused, the last one saying she was too tired. An exasperated Walters pulled his gun and declared, "Damned if I don't see that you do [dance]!" He began shooting holes in the floor at the woman's feet. Johnson and Pipkin, at that point, began shooting, too. The schoolhouse cleared of celebrants in seconds.

Word of the altercation spread quickly and was soon picked up by George Scarborough and Jeff Milton, two occasional lawmen[4] who were out to collect the $500 reward offered by the railroad for the arrest of Walters and each of his companions. Along with a Diamond A cowboy named Martin and a fourth man, Eugene Thacker, they headed for Geronimo where they confirmed that the outlaws were in the area. After scouting around the area for more than two weeks, they came upon a horse camp occupied by six riders and a visiting bear hunter. As a precaution, they disarmed and detained all seven so that the outlaws could not be warned.

Here is what Scarborough himself said happened on the morning of Saturday, July 30: "I saw three men come riding down the hill about three or four hundred yards away. While I was looking at them, two stopped and commenced shooting at a rattlesnake that was under a large rock. The third man, who was in the lead, rode on down towards the camp…. Up to this time I had no idea who the man was, but … I intended to hold him, whoever he might be. He rode up to within thirty feet of where I stood and got off his horse."

The trouble was, at that point Walters recognized Scarborough. He quickly remounted, pulled his pistol and began shooting at the bounty hunter. Scarborough returned fire with a Winchester rifle and Thacker and Milton also opened fire. Badly wounded in the arm and shoulder, Walters tumbled from his horse just as Kid Johnson and Red Pipkin opened fire on the officers from behind a rock some four hundred yards distant. The lawmen laid down a heavy barrage of rifle fire and the outlaws ran for their horses. The officers killed the horses before Johnson and Pipkin could reach them. Johnson tried to take cover behind a tree, but his lower body was exposed and Scarborough shot him through the hip with a .40-70 Winchester. Pipkin escaped over the hill. None of the officers were wounded.

Walters had taken a bullet through the arm and shoulder that lodged in his chest. As he lay unconscious, Milton thought he was dead and began dragging him toward a tent. As he did so, the outlaw coughed up a gob of blood and began gasping for air. Doctors said later that Milton saved Walters' life by breaking up a clot in the outlaw's lungs that had prevented him from breathing.

George Scarborough

Kid Johnson was not so lucky. The bullet that hit him ranged upward into his abdomen, causing him great pain. It was clear that he would die, and it took all day and all night before it happened. Scarborough reported that Johnson's cries of pain could be heard for two miles before he died.

Walters survived his wounds and Scarborough and Milton returned him to New Mexico. In November 1899, he pled guilty to second-degree murder and a Socorro court sentenced him to a life term in the Territorial Penitentiary. He began his sentence on December 14, 1899.

For nearly a dozen years he was a model prisoner. Then, on April 16, 1911 he escaped. Authorities thought he might try to recover the money he'd stashed after the Belen train robbery, and in fact he did head south. Railroad police officers spotted Walters at the village of Isleta and kept him under surveillance for a while. When they became convinced that he was not heading for the money, they took him back into custody and returned him to prison. He served another six years before he was released in April 1917.

Walters assumed the name W. C. Brown and returned to southwestern New Mexico where he found work on the Diamond A ranch. He did return to Alamosa Creek and tried to find the money he'd buried there nearly 20 years before, but he never found it. For years, treasure hunters scoured the area, but they never found the loot, either.[5] Several sources reported that the Alamo Navajos found the paper money not long after it was hidden. One source reports that they spent the money freely, and that it "… smelled like smoke, like it had been in a safe that had been blown by dynamite."

On June 16, 1921, W. C. "Bill" Brown was busy greasing the works on a windmill near Hachita when a dust devil swirled by. Brown was thrown to the ground and lived on but four hours. Bronco Bill may have been about 60 years old. One source says he was born in 1860, another says 1869. They agree that he was born in Texas.

Red Pipkin was captured in March 1899 near Moab, Utah, and returned to Arizona. He served time in Yuma Prison until 1907 on unrelated charges. In 1919 he was sentenced to two years in prison for assault, but only served eight months. In the 1920s, Pipkin became a McKinley County, New Mexico, deputy under Sheriff Bob Roberts. He committed suicide by shooting himself on July 6, 1938 rather than await death from cancer.

ENDNOTES:

[1] The railroads usually reported $250 to $500 taken in any robbery, no matter the actual amount.

[2] One source claims Walters' real name was Walter Brown, and that he was born the son of the sheriff of Brown County, Texas. Brown County never had a sheriff named Brown. Bill Brown is the name Walters used after he was released from prison in 1917.

[3] This William "Kid" Johnson should not be confused with John "Kid" Johnson who participated in the killings of Albuquerque Marshal Bob McGuire and Deputy Marshal E. D. Henry in November 1886. John "Kid" Johnson is

known to have lived well into the 1920s.

[4] At the time, Scarborough was working as a range detective in southwest New Mexico and southeast Arizona although he had previously served as a sheriff in Texas and a deputy U. S. Marshal at El Paso. Jeff Milton was in the employ of Wells Fargo, but took a leave to chase the killers.

[5] In 1990, treasure hunters did find 332 of the silver dollars the gang hid right after the robbery.

SOURCES:

Albuquerque Morning Democrat, May 25, 27 & 28, 1898

Larry D. Ball, *Desert Lawmen, The High Sheriffs of New Mexico and Arizona, 1846-1912*

Howard Bryan, *Robbers, Rogues and Ruffians, True Tales of the Wild West*

Don Bullis, *New Mexico's Finest: Peace Officers Killed in the Line of Duty, 1847-1999*

Robert K. DeArment, *George Scarborough, The Life and Death of A Lawman on the Closing Frontier*

Dan L. Thrapp, *Encyclopedia of Frontier Biography*

Albuquerque, Bernalillo County
1954

City Officer Frank Sjolander Shot, Killed
Officer Gene Casey Badly Wounded
One Offender Dead at Scene, Another Captured

Officer Eugene Casey spotted the car at about an hour after midnight on Wednesday morning, December 1, 1954. It bore Texas plates and matched the description of a car used in several recent armed robberies. It was parked on Gold Avenue near the intersection of Arno Street. Casey radioed Officer Frank Sjolander and asked his help in checking a boarding house at 124 Arno to see if the car's owner could be identified.[1]

Before the officers could knock, the door opened and gunfire erupted. The fight that followed was fast and furious. Both officers were hit but both remained able to return fire. When the smoke cleared both officers were down and so was one of the outlaws, James Leroy Spahr, 22. Spahr was dead. Frank Sjolander died at the hospital about 45 minutes later. Gene Casey was hit five times but survived his wounds.

Investigation revealed that a second shooter along with Spahr was one James Church Isted, aka George Townsend, 21. He fled the scene of the gunfight by jumping out a window and made his way, afoot, to a residence on Lopez Street, southwest, where Lawrence Jay Snow, 20, joined him in flight. Snow was an accomplice in the armed robberies. Both men were California parolees.

The manhunt on December 1 and 2 — some said it was the largest in the history of Albuquerque — soon centered a dozen or so miles south of town, around Isleta Pueblo and Bosque Farms. A railroad shack near Isleta station was found broken into and looted; and the operator of a trading post at Isleta Pueblo positively identified a photograph of Lawrence Snow as the man who had been at the store seeking food. Officers from many different departments and a large contingent of civilians surrounded the Pueblo while Isleta police officers checked buildings on the reservation. No luck.

Things changed on Friday morning. The ground search paid off. A group of five officers came upon a cold campfire. They called for a bloodhound named Symbol and allowed the dog to smell clothing which had been taken from the suspect's Lopez Street house. The animal soon struck the trail and led the officers to the outlaws, who were hiding on a silt island in the middle of an irrigation ditch about two miles south of Isleta. The criminals, under the officer's guns, offered no resistance. They were forced to wade waist-deep in icy cold water from the island to shore. The time was about 11:00 a.m., December 3, 1954. Officer Frank Sjolander's funeral had just concluded.

Once in custody, Isted admitted that he shot officers Sjolander and Casey. Spahr was believed to have fired only one shot before his gun jammed. The weapon, containing seven live rounds, was found under his body. Isted fired eight times, emptying his gun. Isted said he'd smoked marijuana before the shooting, and he was drunk, too.

After a great deal of legal wrangling, Isted's trial date was set for early April. Once the death penalty was taken off the table by District Attorney Paul Tackett, however, Isted enter a plea of guilty to the charges. He was sentenced to life in prison on April 11, 1955.

ENDNOTE:

[1] Another version of the story held that a citizen stopped the officers and told them that there were men with guns inside the address indicated.

SOURCES:

Albuquerque *Journal*, December 2, 3 & 4, 1954; April 12, 1955

Albuquerque *Tribune*, December 10, 1954

Albuquerque Police Department

Don Bullis, *New Mexico's Finest: Peace Officers Killed in the Line of Duty, 1846-1999*

Animas Mountains, Hidalgo County
1932

Customs Man Jay Heard Shot, Killed in Turkey Dispute
Ranchman Claude Gatlin Suspected
Escapes, Dies in Snow Drift

In the early 1930s, Claude Gatlin[1] was named foreman of the Little Hatchet ranch in the boot-heel region of southwestern New Mexico. Among the other livestock Gatlin found at the ranch was a flock of turkeys which belonged to his predecessor, Tom Berkely, and J. H. "Jay" Heard, who was the inspector in charge of the Hachita station of the U.S. Customs Service.[2] The birds were a nuisance to Gatlin because they roosted in the ranch tack shed and left their droppings all over saddles, bridles, and other horse-riding equipment. Gatlin sent word to Inspector Heard to come and get the turkeys. Heard seems to have ignored the request.

After a period of time and further annoyance, Gatlin crated up the birds and hauled them into the community of Hachita where Jay Heard lived. He proceeded to dump them over a fence into Heard's front yard. The inspector heard the racket and confronted Gatlin, and a fight soon followed. Legend holds that Heard administered to Gatlin a sound thrashing.

"Next time I see you," Gatlin said as he left Heard's house, "I'll kill you."

Gatlin's tenure as ranch foreman at the Little Hatchet was short-lived and he was soon fired for drunkenness. He went to stay on a ranch owned by Tom Boles in the Animas Mountains on the Mexican border. Whiskey may have been the common thread in the relationship between Gatlin and Boles, as Boles held his own reputation for drinking and drunkenness.[3]

At about the same time Inspector Heard developed reason to suspect that cattle and horses were being smuggled into the United States from Mexico across the Boles ranch. On Tuesday, June 3, 1932, Heard and another inspector, A. J. "Andy" McKinney, set out to investigate and interview Boles. Gatlin saw them as they drove up to the ranch headquarters in a Ford pickup. He quickly secured an automatic rifle and hid around the corner of the house. As the officers unknowingly approached the house, Gatlin stepped into the open, rifle in hand.

"What are you doing here, Heard?" Gatlin demanded.

Before the officer could respond, Gatlin opened fire. He fired four times, and all four bullets penetrated the windshield of the truck and hit Heard, two in the chest, one in the jaw and one shot away the thumb on the inspector's right hand. Even so, Heard was able to draw his own gun and get off two shots, but both went into the dirt. Inspector McKinney pulled his gun and started in pursuit of Gatlin, but the killer dashed into the house where he used Tom Boles' wife and another woman as shields. Gatlin dared the officers to shoot at him, or to try to enter the house. McKinney and Boles agreed that it would be suicide to try, and in any event, one of the women might well be injured or killed if more shots were fired. They determined that the best immediate course of action was to seek medical help for Inspector Heard. They took him by automobile to Hachita where they put him aboard a passenger train bound for El Paso. One source indicates that Heard died on the train; another that he died in the hospital.

Inspector McKinney notified peace officers from Hachita to Cloverdale in southern Hidalgo County to be on the lookout for Gatlin, and he organized a posse and returned to the Boles ranch to take up a search for the killer. As word of the shooting spread up and down the Animas Valley, other posses were mounted and took up pursuit. They scoured the rugged and desolate country along the Mexican border for miles in either direction for several days. Gatlin made good his escape and was never captured and prosecuted for the crime.

Gatlin did not disappear from history, however. He remained in Mexico, living a "squalid" life, according to one source, and returning to the United States on thieving raids. He also seems to have kept up with his drinking ways. He died from exposure one night, drunk, in a snow bank, in northern Mexico.

ENDNOTES:

[1] One source identifies this subject as Claude Gatliff. Probably a typographical error.

[2] J. H. Heard was a mounted Customs rider. These officers were sometimes called outriders. One source incorrectly refers to him as a Border Patrol Officer.

[3] In February 1937, Tom Boles, while drunk, shot up the town of Hachita. Deputy Sheriff John Hall shot him in the arm when he "menaced" the officer. The bullet broke the cattleman's arm and he was later charged with resisting an officer, flourishing a deadly weapon and discharging firearms within a settlement.

SOURCES:

Albuquerque *Journal*, May 3, 1932
Deming *Graphic*, May 5, 1932
El Paso *Times*, May 3, 1932
George Hilliard, *Adios Hachita, Stories of a New Mexico Town*
Roger Payne, Deputy Chief, New Mexico State Police (Ret.)
Silver City *Daily Press*, February 22, 1937

Joseph Callaway Lea and Lincoln County Sheriff John Poe. Courtesy Historical Society of Southeast New Mexico, no. 3326-J.

24

Anton Chico, Guadalupe County
1884 & 1885

Horse Thief Kills Lincoln County Deputies
In Separate Gunfights
Captured After Siege — Jailed

In early 1884 Nicholas Aragon and another man, both from San Miguel County, New Mexico, stole several horses along the Rio Hondo in Lincoln County and removed them to a canyon near Anton Chico on the Rio Pecos, south of Las Vegas. Lincoln County authorities learned where the horses were hidden and Deputy Sheriff Jim Brent and a posse soon recovered the animals, captured Aragon and his friend, and jailed them in Lincoln. Aragon escaped from jail on May 28 by climbing through a hole in the roof. In October of the same year, Sheriff John Poe[1] learned that Aragon had been seen in his old haunts around Gallinas Springs and Anton Chico in San Miguel County. Sheriff Poe told Deputy Sheriff Jasper Corn of Roswell[2] to take as many men as he needed to arrest the horse thief.

Corn took only one man: his brother-in-law, Bill Holloman[3]. He soon learned that Aragon regularly visited a particular woman near

25

Anton Chico and they approached her house. The outlaw saw Deputy Corn coming and dashed out the back door, running for his horse that stood saddled and waiting some distance away, beyond a stone fence. Corn, from horseback, opened fire with his pistol as his mount galloped toward Aragon. Aragon, using the fence for cover, returned fire with a Winchester rifle. His first shot struck Corn's horse in the neck, knocking the animal down, and the deputy with it. Even though Corn was pinned to the ground, his leg caught under the horse and badly broken, he continued the fight until his gun was empty. Aragon took his time, then aimed carefully, and shot Corn in the stomach. Aragon mounted his horse and escaped before Holloman could stop him. Corn suffered greatly and died thirty-six hours later without ever receiving medical treatment.

Aragon hid out for a few months and then, once again, returned to Anton Chico. In late January 1885, Sheriff Poe led a posse made up of Jim Brent, Johnny Hurley, Barney Mason, Billy Bufer and Jim Abercrombie in search of the killer. A little investigation led the posse to a house where Aragon was believed to be hiding. Two women living there said they were alone in the house; that Aragon was not there. Sheriff Poe assigned Deputy Hurley—who spoke fluent Spanish—to take the women into the kitchen and interrogate them carefully while the remainder of the posse surrounded the house. After a while, one of the women admitted that Aragon was in the house. She said the fugitive was heavily armed and ready to fight. In his haste to tell the sheriff that Aragon was there, Hurley allowed himself to be silhouetted in the kitchen door.

"We've got him! He's in there!" Hurley called out to Sheriff Poe.

"Johnny, get out from in front of the door or he'll kill you," Poe yelled just as Aragon fired.

"Are you hit, Johnny?" Poe asked.

"Yes," the deputy replied. "Gut shot."

Hurley staggered back into the kitchen and lay down before the fire. The women made him as comfortable as possible. He died 36 hours later just as Corn survived for 36 hours after Aragon shot him in the stomach. He, too, received no medical attention.

In the meantime, gunfire became general between Aragon inside the house, and the posse outside. Though badly wounded in three places—in the head and leg—the outlaw managed to hold off his pursuers for more than sixty hours. Aragon didn't surrender until the sheriff from Las Vegas, Hilario Romero, arrived and promised the outlaw he would not be harmed.

Sheriff Poe and Deputy Brent took Aragon to Santa Fe and lodged him in jail there.[4] Aragon was tried during the summer of 1885 and acquitted on charges of murdering Jasper Corn. Aragon's argument was that he didn't know Corn was a deputy, and that Corn fired first. In the fall of 1885, a Colfax County jury found Aragon guilty of second-degree murder for killing Johnny Hurley and gave him a life sentence.[5] He actually served about 10 years before he was released and returned to Anton Chico, where he died of natural causes many years later.

ENDNOTES:

[1] John W. Poe succeeded Pat Garrett as sheriff of Lincoln County. James Brent succeeded him.

[2] Roswell was in Lincoln County at the time. Chaves County was not created until 1889.

[3] The name may have been spelled *Holliman*. One source identifies William Holliman as married to Zilpha Corn, Martin Corn's sister. Judge Smith Lea in Klasner's book identified Bill Holliman as Jasper Corn's brother-in-law. It is logical to assume that Martin and Jasper Corn were brothers.

[4] One source says Aragon was held in the Territorial Penitentiary, but that is unlikely since New Mexico's first prison didn't open until August 1885.

[5] A later reporter held that Aragon was acquitted of killing Hurley and convicted of killing Corn. Lily Klasner, who was alive at the time, told the story related here. It seems most creditable.

[6] One historian claims that Aragon killed both Hurley and Corn as he escaped from jail in Lincoln. There seems to be little support for that version of the story.

SOURCES:

Don Bullis, *New Mexico's Finest: Peace Officers Killed in the Line of Duty, 1847-1999*

Fred Harrison, *Hell Holes and Hangings*

H. B. Henning, Ed., *George Curry, 1861-1947, An Autobiography*

Lily Klasner, *My Girlhood Among Outlaws*

Carole Larson, *Forgotten Frontier*

Lincoln, *Golden Era*, February 5, 1885, October 1, 1885

Santa Fe *Daily New Mexican*, July 16 & 17, 1885

John P. Wilson, *Merchants, Guns & Money, The Story of Lincoln County and Its Wars*

Black Mountains, Socorro County
1911

*Luna County Jail Escapees Kill Deputies
In Wild Gun Fight – One Outlaw Killed
A Second Hanged at Socorro*

When the Mexican Revolution began in 1910, many North Americans went south to fight on the side of the rebels under Francisco I. Madero. Among them were brothers John and Reynold Greer and Irvin Frazier.

The three of them participated in the March 1911 battle at Casas Grandes in northern Chihuahua during which rebel forces were defeated by federal troops. In the course of the fighting, John Greer received serious bullet wounds to his head and body and was left behind on the battlefield as the rebels retreated and federal troops advanced. Irvin Frazier rode to his rescue. Firing his rifle until it was empty, Frazier was able to hold off the soldiers long enough to get Greer onto his horse, and the two rode to safety. They soon crossed the border into the United States and Frazier remained with Greer in a mountain cabin until the wounded man recovered. Greer promised Frazier that

29

he would repay the favor, with his own life if necessary.

In November of the same year, John Greer was given an opportunity to make good on his pledge.

Irvin Frazier, using the name John Gates, was arrested for burglary and held in the Luna County Jail at Deming, New Mexico. He got word to his friend, John Greer, that he needed help in escaping. On the night of November 7, 1911, a masked man climbed over the wall at the jail and held Sheriff Dwight B. Stephens and two deputies at gunpoint. He stole their guns and freed Frazier. A third man, also masked, waited with three horses outside the wall. They all made it safely away from the jail.

Sheriff Stephens and a posse made of deputies Tom Hall, A. L. Smithers, Johnnie James and W. C. Simpson took up pursuit. The chase took eight days during which the outlaws were able to provision themselves by robbing ranch houses along the way. Finally, late on the afternoon of November 18, the posse caught up with the outlaws at an adobe house on the VXT ranch in the Black Mountains of Socorro County. As the posse surrounded the place, the outlaws mounted their horses and rode out, single file, as if to meet the officers. Suddenly, at a distance of fifty or so yards, they stopped and quickly dismounted, drawing guns as they did so, as if in a military maneuver. Then they opened fire, shooting both Deputies Hall and Smithers. Smithers fell dead in his tracks, shot through the body. Hall was able to empty his Winchester rifle before he, too, fell mortally wounded from a bullet in the head. The killers remounted and attempted to flee.

Sheriff Stephens, who had taken a position on the opposite side of the house, hurried into the fight. He shot John Greer as bullets hit all around him, and both Reynold Greer and Irvin Frazier again jumped from their horses and fled into an *arroyo* on foot, firing as they went. Deputy Simpson arrived on the scene and opened fire on Frazier with some success, and, though wounded, the outlaw made good his escape, as did Reynold Greer. John Greer, 19, died at the scene of the fight.

Sheriff Stephens and what remained of his posse abandoned the chase and took the three bodies to the railroad at Engles, 85 miles to the east.

The *Deming Headlight* eulogized deputies Hall and Smithers in this way:

> Thos. H. Hall and E. L. Smithers [sic], as truly heroes as ever went forth in the defense of law and justice have died a martyr's death. A home in Deming is desolate. A wife and mother's heart is bleeding at every pore. Five orphan children, four manly sons and a noble daughter are bowed in grief and go forth into the world to battle without the counsel, and strong protecting arm of a father.

A few weeks later, a man using the name John Gates, hungry and desperate, attempted to pawn a pistol in El Paso, Texas. Engraved on the butt of the weapon was the name of the man from whom Luna County Sheriff Dwight Stephens had acquired it. Gates was shortly arrested and identified as Irvin Frazier. He was promptly returned to Socorro where he was tried for the murders of Tom Hall and A. L. Smithers. Convicted of the crimes, he was sentenced to death by hanging.

During his time in the state penitentiary awaiting execution, he was able to smuggle out a letter to Reynold Greer in which he detailed the best way for Greer to rescue him as he was being transferred from Santa Fe to the gallows in Socorro[1]. His suggestion was that Greer board the train in Albuquerque and set up a trap at La Joya. Officers learned of the letter and took appropriate measures, but no effort was made to deliver Frazier from his date with the hangman. Reynold Greer was never captured.

Captain Fred Fornoff of the New Mexico Mounted Police, Socorro County Sheriff Emil James, Eddy County Sheriff Miles Cicero Stewart and 15 or so additional deputies, armed with rifles and shotguns, transferred Frazier and another killer, Francisco Grando, from Santa Fe to Socorro in the early morning hours of April 25, 1913. Along the way, Frazier told Sheriff Stewart that he hadn't killed either of the Luna County deputies. He said both officers were down before he ever fired a shot. The condemned men were taken to the courthouse

New Mexico Mounted Police
Captain Fred Fornoff

and held there briefly before they were removed to a gallows which amounted to a trapdoor placed in the floor of a second story room in the jail. Frazier asked for a drink of whiskey. Fornoff refused. Frazier's final words were, "Get that noose tight, boys. Have as little pain to this as possible."

At exactly 5:42 a.m., the trapdoor dropped open and Frazier came to the end of his rope. A doctor declared him dead 12 minutes later. He was 26 years old.

Sheriff Dwight Stephens was himself killed by jail escapees in February of 1916.

ENDNOTE:

[1] Each New Mexico county carried out its own executions by hanging until 1929 when the state, by law, assumed the responsibility. The state first used the electric chair in 1933.

SOURCES:

Albuquerque *Morning Journal*, November 20, 1911, April 25, 26, 1913
Associated Press, April 25, 1913
Deming *Headlight*, November 24, 1911

Bluitt, Roosevelt County
1932

Gun Fight with Bank Robbers
At Rural Homestead
Texas Lawman Killed – Deputy Wounded

On July 15, 1932, a band of three or four robbers held up the bank at Olton, Lamb County, Texas. They made off with about $3,800. An investigation by Lamb County Sheriff Bob Crim produced suspects Lee Pebworth, Glen Hunsucker and Jack Sullivan. The sheriff secured arrest warrants for the three and organized a posse made up of himself, Deputies Harve Bolin and Bob Miller, District Attorney Meade F. Griffin, and Roosevelt County, New Mexico, Deputy R. L. Hollis.[1]

Crim's investigation led him to Lee Pebworth's ramshackle homestead located near the village of Bluitt in far-southern Roosevelt County, between the communities of Milnesand, New Mexico and Bledsoe, Texas. Early in the morning hours of Saturday, August 20, 1932, the posse took up positions near the farmhouse. As four men walked from the farmhouse to the barn, Sheriff Crim identified himself and ordered them to "...stick up your hands!" Instead of obeying, the outlaws produced guns—Pebworth secured a rifle he'd previously hidden in a feed trough—and commenced firing at the officers.

Deputies Bolin and Hollis went down with the first volley. Shot in the head, Bolin died immediately. Shot in the mouth and hip, Hollis was severely wounded, but survived. The officers took cover and returned fire. Pebworth was wounded but, along with three other bandits, managed to escape from the scene.

Police departments and sheriff's offices all over eastern New Mexico and West Texas were alerted to be on the lookout for the killers. At about noon the same day, Sheriff Bob Beverly of Lea County, New Mexico, and a posse arrested Pebworth and Stanley Headrick at the Dalmont ranch, about 12 miles southwest of Tatum. Pebworth's wound prevented his escape. No trace of the remaining outlaws was immediately found. Headrick was arrested but claimed that he had no part in the shooting. Pebworth's son-in-law, Joe Jones, was also arrested, and he too claimed innocence. Charges against Headrick and Jones were subsequently dropped. Jack Sullivan and Glen Hunsucker disappeared completely.

Texas and New Mexico officers shot and seriously wounded Sullivan before they arrested him near Mountainair, in Torrance County three weeks later on September 13, 1932. Texas authorities extradited him for the robbery of the Olton bank. He was held in the Lubbock County jail, from which he escaped on November 19, 1932. Recaptured at Vernon, Texas, just before Christmas, he was subsequently tried and convicted of the Olton robbery and an armed robbery he committed during his escape, and sentenced to 37 years in prison. He was not tried for the killing of Harve Bolin.

Glenn Hunsucker was shot and killed by a Lincoln County, New Mexico, posse in July of 1933 between Ramon and Corona. Before his death, he'd participated in the killings of four peace officers: Harve Bolin; Sheriff John Moseley of Swisher County, Texas; Deputy Sheriff Joe Brown of Wise County, Texas; and Chief Deputy Sheriff Tom Jones of Lincoln County, New Mexico.

On October 5, 1932 Lee Pebworth, about 60 years old, appeared before a Portales judge and pleaded guilty to second-degree murder with the understanding that he would not receive the death penalty. He was sentenced to 99 years in prison. He actually served about nine years before he was paroled. He died soon afterward.

ENDNOTE:

[1] Different sources tell different stories about the number of possemen that participated in the battle at Pebworth's farm. One source indicates the group was seven strong. Most likely, the members were Sheriff Crim, Harve Bolin, Meade Griffin, and R. L. Hollis. Deputy Bob Miller may have been there — he said he was — but some sources do not mention him. Dozens of officers participated in the search for the killers.

SOURCES:

Albuquerque *Journal*, August 21, September 14, December 21, 1932

Don Bullis, *New Mexico's Finest: Peace Officers Killed in the Line of Duty, 1847-1999*

Carlsbad *Current-Argus*, August 20, September 14, 1932

Clovis *Evening News*, August 22, 1932

Lubbock, Texas, *Sunday Avalanche Journal*, August 21, 1932

Plainview, Texas, *Evening Herald*, August 21 & 22, 1932

Roswell *Morning Dispatch*, October 5, 1932

New Mexico Department of Corrections records

Carlsbad, Eddy County
1897

*Former County Sheriff Kemp Shoots, Kills
Current Sheriff Dow on Eddy Street:
Kemp Claims Innocence*

David Lyle Kemp[1] was born in Hamilton, Hamilton County,[2] Texas, southwest of Fort Worth, on March 1, 1862, to William A. and Mary Jane Snow Kemp. He had five full brothers and sisters and one half-brother, Walker Bush, who was six years his senior.[3]

Kemp's first fatal gunfight occurred on the streets of Hamilton in 1887 when he was 15 years old. Men named Bogan and Smith began shooting at each other and young Kemp became involved, killing Daniel Smith. Sheriff G. N. Gentry attempted to intercede and Kemp tried to shoot him, too, but his gun misfired and Kemp was arrested. He was tried, convicted and sentenced to hang.

If he'd kept his date with the hangman, the story would end here. Two of his sisters, it is reported, had married prominent men and they used their influence to Dave's benefit; and ultimately his death sentence was not only commuted, but Governor Richard Hubbard pardoned him. One source states that Kemp had provided the warden with "valuable information" and that may have contributed to the clemency. Another source says this was entirely appropriate since Dave only acted in self-defense. He left Texas upon being freed.

By the late 1880s Kemp was living at Eddy, in southeastern New Mexico. He is said to have dealt in horses and other livestock, operated a butcher shop, been a partner in a drug store and in a saloon. More specifically, he and Tom Gray operated the Lone Wolf saloon. In 1888 he married Elizabeth King and they had a son, Joseph Clyde, born in 1889.

Dark rumors spread around Eddy alleging nefarious deeds related to Kemp's saloon business and his activities in the livestock trade. Nothing was ever proved and he was never arrested or charged, and none of it prevented his being elected sheriff when Eddy County was created in 1890. Some sources have said that he operated the sheriff's department in a way that benefited his friends in the saloon business. It is certainly true that the sin village of Phenix [sic], south of Eddy, prospered during his term, but it seems unlikely that he alone would have been responsible for it. In fact, Kemp's temperance was well known. The Eddy County *Argus* said this:

> Now that Dave Kemp has been elected sheriff, it is hoped that he will quit chewing gum, which is the only bad habit he has. He is perhaps the only sheriff-elect in New Mexico Territory that does not use tobacco, drink liquor, or indulge in profanity.

Kemp's term of office was uneventful, with one exception. In July 1893, he arrested one James Barrett for a double murder committed near Seven Rivers. Kemp, assisted by Walker Bush, also oversaw Barrett's hanging in September of the following year, the only hanging in Eddy County history.

Kemp could not succeed himself after two terms in office, and he endorsed Walker Bush in the 1894 election. Bush lost to John Walker. Walker appointed Kemp his deputy and served a single term, losing to Les Dow in 1896.

Eddy County Sheriff James Leslie "Les" Dow. Photograph courtesy of the author.

James Leslie Dow was also born in Texas, at Clinton in DeWitt County, southeast of San Antonio in 1860. He became a deputy U. S. Marshal at an early age and he married Molly Neatherlin in 1884. That same year the Southwestern Livestock Association hired him as an inspector. His job was to help solve the enormous cattle-rustling problem then plaguing southern New Mexico and West Texas. He arrived at Seven Rivers, New Mexico, about 20 miles north of Eddy, in 1885. He owned a ranch there, west of the town, and he soon opened the Seven Rivers Saloon.

In early April 1891, a ne'er-do-well and drunkard named Zack Light accosted Dow in his bar and demanded money. When Dow declined, Light pulled his gun, but his shot went high. Dow's did not. He killed Light on the spot. He was acquitted on a plea of self-defense.

Dow developed a reputation as a persistent and fearless lawman. It was he who was largely responsible for the indictments of Oliver Lee, Jim Gilliland and Bill McNew for cattle theft. As a result of this case, Prosecutor Albert Jennings Fountain and his young son, Henry, were murdered at the Chalk Hills, east of Las Cruces, in February 1896.

J. D. Walker ran for re-election in 1896, but Les Dow defeated him and took office on January 1, 1897. Dow immediately targeted Kemp. He seemed to believe that the former sheriff was responsible for some of the cattle thefts in the area. In early February Dow arrested Kemp for carrying a gun.

On the evening of February 18, 1897, it all came to a head. Les Dow walked out of the post office and was shot in the face at close range. He died the next morning at about 7:00 o'clock.

One version of the story goes that Kemp and another man, Will Kennon, hid in a doorway near the post office and simply waited for Dow to come out the door. When the sheriff did so, Kemp shot him and fled. Dee Harkey, a constable, arrived within a few minutes. Harkey said that Dow could not identify his assailant because the muzzle flash from the gun, so close to his face, temporarily blinded him. Harkey believed that Kemp was the guilty party. The constable, however, didn't like either man, and oddly enough helped Kemp avoid a sheriff's posse later the same evening.[5] (Note: Harkey's version of events is taken from his autobiography, *Mean As Hell*, which is generally considered unreliable as an historical source.)

Miles Cicero Stewart, also one of Dow's enemies, claimed that Dow drew first and challenged Kemp, who then pulled his gun and shot the sheriff.[6] Another witness. W. H. Smith, claimed that there was a confrontation between the two men and when they went for their guns, Dow's hung up in the holster giving Kemp the opportunity to shoot him.

Whatever really happened, Dave Kemp was acquitted of murdering Dow in a trial held at Roswell — on a change of venue — in March 1898.

Kemp remained a resident of Eddy for some years. He continued to deal in livestock and stayed in the saloon business. He and Elizabeth were divorced and he married Ada Patti in April 1898.[4] None of the children of his second marriage survived to adolescence. His father, who had resided in Eddy since 1891, died in 1903. After 15 or so years, Dave decided it was time for a move, which took him to Lipscomb County at the far north end of the Texas Panhandle. He bought ranch land there and in Beaver County, Oklahoma.

One of the schemes he worked on in his later life was the development of a town called LaKemp, Oklahoma. It didn't succeed because he could not get the railroad to route a track to the community. What there was of the place moved to Booker, Texas in 1919. Kemp also served on the Booker school board and occasionally as a deputy sheriff. He never again resorted to the use of his gun, but one source says he did engage in fisticuffs a time or two as the years went by.

Legend held that Kemp's sister killed him, but that is not so. On the morning of January 4, 1935, he dropped dead of a massive heart attack. He was 72 years old.

Dave died blameless of any criminal act, so far as the law was concerned. His single act of deviltry seems to have been the shooting of Les Dow, and it is unlikely that anyone will ever know what *really* happened on that winter day in 1897.

ENDNOTES:

[1] One source cited his name as David *Leon*. Mrs. Sara Bush Hendricks, Kemp's great-granddaughter, asserted that his correct middle name was *Lyle*. Throughout his adult life he was called "Dave," "D. L." or, in some cases, "Mr. Kemp."

[2] Other sources have claimed he was born in Coleman County, Texas.

[3] Mrs. Hendricks points out that documentation is lacking which would prove that Mary Jane Snow was ever married to a man named Bush. She was, however, identified in official documents as Walker Bush's mother.

[4] One source provides this information. The genealogical chart of the Kemp family provided by Mrs. Hendricks shows Dave's second wife as Mary Asbury, as do other sources. No mention is made of Ada Patti, although it is likely that he married three times. This same source claims that Kemp's mother died in 1900. Mrs. Hendricks' chart shows that Mary Jane Snow died in 1875.

SOURCES:

West Gilbreath, *Death on the Gallows*

Dee Harkey, *Mean As Hell*

Sara Bush Hendricks, conversations

Dennis McCown, "The Last Shooting in the Old West," *Quarterly of the National Association for Outlaw and Lawman History*

Leon Metz, *The Encyclopedia of Lawmen, Outlaws, and Gunfighters*

Bill O'Neal, "They Called Him MISTER Kemp," *True West*, April 1991

Cimarron, Colfax County
1875

Clay Allison: Noted Shootist
Killer & Drunkard
Left Mark on New Mexico

(Note: Writing about historical figures who lived on the American Frontier as it moved ever westward is a trying task. Much has been written on many of them, but few of their biographers agree upon the details of their lives. The case of Clay Allison is a good example.)

Robert Clay Allison called himself a shootist, and he was. Writers on the Old West generally agree on that point, but little else about the man or his life. A look at a few sources will provide readers with three or four different Clay Allisons.

Try these four books: *The Gunfighters* by the editors of Time-Life Books with text by Paul Trachtman; *The Gunfighters* with paintings and text by Lea Franklin McCarty; *The Album of Gunfighters* by J. Marvin Hunter and Noah H. Rose; and the *Encyclopedia of Western Gunfighters*, by Bill O'Neal. A word on these sources: Trachtman is comprehensive

Robert A. "Clay" Allison

and readable McCarty is exactly the opposite. He claims to have known a man who knew Wyatt Earp. No other sources are cited. Hunter and Rose are generally considered reliable and so is O'Neal.

All four sources agree that Allison was born in Tennessee, *probably* at or near Waynesboro in 1840. From this point on the departures are many. Take his military career for instance.

The Album of Gunfighters says this: "… [He] became a [Confederate] spy. He was captured and sentenced to be shot, but killed his two guards and escaped the night before he was to be executed." That's pretty exciting stuff.

The McCarty book reports, "… [He] had been a soldier in the Confederate Army where he learned about easy-go killing. As a guerrilla he became adept at the art of gunslinging." None of that seems to make sense.

The Time-Life book says, "When the Civil War began, [Allison] enlisted in the Tennessee Light Artillery. Three months later he was given a medical discharge by … army doctors; they described him as 'incapable of performing the duties of a soldier because of a blow received many years ago.' Emotional or physical excitement produces paroxysmals of mixed character, partly epileptic and partly maniacal."

O'Neal says this: "At the outbreak of the Civil War, Allison ignored his clubfoot and defended his native state, serving throughout the conflict in various Confederate units." O'Neal is the only source to report that Allison had a clubfoot.

The tombstone at the head of Allison's grave indicates that he served in Co. F., 9th Tennessee Cavalry. It also identified him as a "Gentleman Gun Fighter."

So much for Allison's military career.

Sources generally agree that he left Tennessee after the Civil War and migrated first to Texas and then on to Colfax County, New Mexico, with stops in Colorado and Kansas along the way. In 1870, a Missouri newspaper alleged that Allison had already killed 15 men. Allison replied, "I have at all times tried to use my influence toward protecting the property holders and substantial men of the country from thieves,

outlaws, and murderers, among whom I do not care to be classed."
Note that he did not deny killing 15, or any other number, of men.

Despite his protestations of respectability, people living in Colfax
County knew him for what he was: not only a killer, but also a man
who took perverse pleasure in killing.

Only the Hunter/Rose book says that Allison killed 18 men in his
lifetime, and even they point out that the figure is based on Allison's
reputation, and not documented fact. Other sources do not offer a total.
Research indicates that he killed at least three or four men, and participated in the killings of several others. Eighteen is an unlikely number.

Trachtman and O'Neal tell variations on the following story. A man
named Kennedy was accused of killing several strangers and his own
infant daughter. He was arrested and taken to jail at Elizabethtown,
New Mexico. Some bones were found at Kennedy's cabin several days
later, but they were determined to not be human in origin. No matter. Allison and some of his drunken friends judged Kennedy guilty
and sentenced him to death. In October 1870, they broke into the jail
and removed the condemned man to a nearby slaughterhouse where
they lynched him. That wasn't enough for Allison. He decapitated the
corpse, mounted the head on a long stick, and then rode to Cimarron
where he carried the grisly trophy into Lambert's saloon. This is an
unlikely story since the Lambert Saloon didn't open in Cimarron until
1872, well after the above events.

Another event in Allison's life shows something of the nature of
"gunfighting" in the Old West. The McCarthy book says that a man
by the name of William Chunk arrived in town one day with the ex-
pressed purpose of killing Allison. But instead of going into the street
and shooting at one another, the two men went into a restaurant for
dinner. During the course of the meal, Allison is said to have become
annoyed at Chunk's table manners and killed the man for eating salad
with his mouth open.

Time-Life agrees that the man probably intended to kill Allison, but
his name was not William Chunk, but Chunk Colbert (all other sources
agree about the name), and he was the nephew of a man Allison had

fought years earlier. The two did go to dinner. When coffee was being served, Colbert attempted to kill Allison by pulling his gun from under the table. His gun barrel struck the edge of the table, however, and his shot went wide, deflected by the wood. Allison then calmly pulled his own gun and shot Colbert in the forehead, killing him instantly. Asked later why he would take a meal with a man who meant to kill him, Allison said, "Because I didn't want to send a man to hell on an empty stomach."

O'Neal says the fight between Allison and Colbert resulted from a contested horse race.

One would imagine that a man such as Allison would die by the gun, as he had lived. Not so. He was killed when run over by a freight wagon. Sources, again, do not agree as to the details. *The Album of Gunfighters* reports that his team ran away and in the process Allison was thrown under the wagon wheels and his neck broken. McCarthy says the wagon struck a chuckhole, which caused Allison to drop the reins and fall off and be run over, breaking his back. Time-Life says Allison was hauling supplies to his ranch when a bag of grain slipped. He reached for it, lost his balance and fell off the wagon, was run over and killed. O'Neal says he fractured his skull on a wheel when he fell off the wagon, and died an hour later. (A fifth source agrees that he fractured his skull, but claims the wagon hit a clump of salt grass, throwing Allison from the seat.) The less reverential among history writers suggest that drunkenness may have contributed to the fall from the wagon box which led to Allison's death.

And when? McCarthy says it happened in 1877. Other sources agree that the year was 1887. Two of them say July 1, and one of them asserts Allison died on July 3.

Here is what one newspaper editor had to say on the occasion of Allison's death:

> "Certain it is that many of his stern deeds were for the right as he understood it to be." Damned by faint praise, it seems.

A second tombstone at the foot of Allison's grave reads, "He never killed a man that did not need killing."

ADDITIONAL SOURCES:

Richard Melzer, *Buried Treasures, Famous and Unusual Gravesites in New Mexico*
Chuck Parsons, *Clay Allison, Portrait of a Shootist*
Dan L. Thrapp, *Encyclopedia of Frontier Biography*

Cimarron, Colfax County
1876

David Crockett, Kin of Famed
Alamo Fighter
Bites the Dust in Drunken Affray

It doesn't matter much that some debunkers have attempted to show that David Crockett of Tennessee didn't die bravely at the Alamo in Texas on March 6, 1836, but rather surrendered and was ingloriously executed by Mexican soldiers under General Antonio Lopez de Santa Anna. He remains a national—and Texas—hero nonetheless. The same cannot be said for his grandson, and namesake[1].

After Texas independence was gained later in 1836 with Sam Houston's victory over General Santa Anna at San Jacinto (April 21), the new government awarded Crockett's widow, Elizabeth, some property along the Brazos River in what is now Hood County, southwest of Fort Worth. Robert Crockett, the elder Davy's son, and his wife Matilda moved to Texas from Tennessee in the mid-1850s. With the couple was their son David "Davy," who had been born in February 1853. Robert Crockett operated a toll bridge over the Brazos.

47

No one is certain when young Davy arrived in Cimarron, Colfax County, New Mexico. Some sources place him in New Mexico as early as 1870 when he is said to have participated — along with famed "shootist" Clay Allison — in the lynching of Charles Kennedy[2] who, according to legend, was decapitated and his head taken to the Lambert Saloon in Cimarron. Other sources discount this tale. "…A mob led by Allison and Crockett could not have been…possible. The Lambert Saloon was not in existence until 1872. Crockett was not yet in New Mexico, but in Texas."[3] Crockett would have only been 17 years old at the time.

Historians generally agree that Crockett operated a small ranch near Cimarron by the mid-1870s. One of his neighbors was Clay Allison; another was Pete Burleson, with whom Crocket had been acquainted in Texas. Crockett's ranch foreman was Gus Heffron[4]. It is also generally agreed that Crockett was a likeable young man, and well received at local social events. Gus Heffron was exactly the opposite, considered by townsmen as a quarrelsome braggart and coward. All the same, Crockett and Heffron struck up a strong friendship.

The first of Crockett's assaults upon society took place on March 24, 1876 in the barroom of the St. James Hotel. The story goes that Crockett, Heffron and a third man, Henry Goodman, had spent the day drinking in Cimarron's saloons and that evening they stopped at the St. James to get one more bottle of booze to take with them, back to the ranch. Crockett had trouble leaving the establishment, as the door wouldn't seem to open. He discovered that the cause was a soldier, a Black soldier, on the other side of the portal, trying to get in. Crockett pulled his gun and shot the man dead, then whirled and shot three other Black soldiers who were sitting at a table and playing cards. Two of them died[5].

Crockett later surrendered himself to a friendly court where he plead his innocence predicated on the notion that it was simply a matter of drunken behavior with no malice involved. The court agreed and fined Crockett $50 for "carrying arms."[6]

At some point, Crockett decided that cattle ranching was not for him, so he sold off his livestock and spent his time in hoorawing the town of Cimarron. Along with Heffron, he was often observed riding up and down the town's main street firing his pistol into the air, or taking casual shots at random targets. The county's new sheriff, Isaiah Rinehart, who had taken office on March 8, seemed powerless to stop the depredations.

On one occasion, Crockett was said to have roped a pedestrian, dragged him to the general store and outfitted him with a new suit of clothes, the bill for which he sent to Sheriff Rinehart. Another time, the story goes, he forced the sheriff, at the point of a gun, to drink whiskey until the lawman was completely intoxicated. This behavior went on for six months. But Sheriff Rinehart and the people of Cimarron had had enough.

Late in September 1876, Crockett and Heffron were again in Cimarron on a drunken spree and making nuisances of themselves. On Saturday the 30th, Sheriff Rinehart approached a rancher named Joseph Holbrook and postmaster John McCullough and asked them to arm themselves and assist him in arresting Crockett and Heffron. They agreed. Late that afternoon the lawmen approached the drunken revelers, who were mounted and on the road out of town. Holbrook ordered them to stop. A drunken Crockett apparently did not take the officers seriously and told them to go ahead and shoot. They did! When the shots were fired, Crockett's horse bolted. When it was found some time later, Crockett was still aboard, shot dead, his hand gripping the saddle horn so strongly that his fingers had to be pried loose.

Heffron, wounded in the head, escaped only to be captured later. He then broke out of jail and disappeared from history. Sheriff Rinehart and his deputies were tried and acquitted of any crime associated with the killing of Crockett.

Pete Burleson, Crockett's friend from Texas, took charge of the outlaw's body and had it laid out in a Cimarron rooming house. Burleson is said to have been outraged when Rinehart, Holbrook and McCullough entered the room without removing their hats. One source says he had to be physically restrained. He must have stayed angry. Just over a month later Burleson was elected sheriff of Colfax County.

It seems likely that even a maverick like the elder Davy Crockett would not have been proud of his grandson.

ENDNOTES:

[1] One source reports that the younger Davy Crockett was the nephew of the one who died at the Alamo. Other sources generally agree that he was the grandson of the hero.

[2] Kenney was an alleged multi-murderer who made a practice of killing travelers and burying their bodies near his home.

[3] *Clay Allison, Portrait of a Shootist*, by Chuck Parsons.

[4] The name has been variously spelled as Hefferson, Heffner, and Heifner.

[5] One source lists the three soldiers killed as Privates George Small, John Hanson and Anthony Harvey, members of Troop "L", 9th Cavalry, better known as Buffalo Soldiers.

[6] This crime is often attributed to Clay Allison, but he was not present when the soldiers were killed.

SOURCES:

Larry D. Ball, *Desert Lawmen, The High Sheriffs of New Mexico & Arizona 1846-1912*

Howard Bryan, *Robbers, Rogues, and Ruffians: True Tales of the Wild West*

Leon Claire Metz, *The Encyclopedia of Lawmen, Outlaws and Gunfighters*

Corrales, Sandoval County
1898

Murder of Estranged Wife
Gunfight with Lawmen
Claims Life of French Winemaker

An old adobe structure in Corrales was for generations known as the Territorial House or simply as the T-House.[1] It is one of the older structures in the village, dating back to the early 19th century. History holds that it was constructed between 1801 and 1809[2]. The building was originally a residence.

Ownership of the Territorial House over the years is somewhat uncertain. Both official and oral histories are incomplete, contradictory and confusing. It seems reasonably certain that the building and 25 to 30 acres around it were purchased by a French grape-grower and winemaker named Luis Emberto and his wife, Louisa, in the middle 1880s. Rosie Armijo of Corrales, who has researched the matter, indicates that the winemaker's name was Louis Imbert. The confusion may arise in translating the name from French to Spanish to English.

Florencio Garcia, a life-long Corrales resident, told the tragic Embertos tale to Robert Gilliland sometime prior to 1975, when Mr. Gilliland died.[3] Mr. Garcia was 88 years old at the time.

In the late 1880s and early 1890s, Luis and Louisa were quite prosperous. They planted an orchard as well as grapes and Mr. Garcia said, "the fruit could not be imitated." The peaches were freestone and as large as a cup. They sold their fruit in Albuquerque. The Embertos were also popular in the Corrales community. They entertained frequently and lavishly and their home was a favorite gathering place for local residents.

But in May of 1893, things changed for them. Their son, Luis Jr., about 10 years old at the time, was playing with a rifle (perhaps a shotgun used to kill snakes) with some other boys in what became the dining room at the north end of the building. A lady named Dolores (Lola) Griego was busy hanging grapes from ceiling *vigas*. Young Luis Jr. at one point said he was going to kill Mrs. Griego, and then he shot her to death. Mr. Garcia said the matter was investigated, but he failed to mention the outcome except to say that the boys thought the gun was not loaded.

After that, the quality of life for the Embertos seemed to decline. Luis and Louisa frequently fought, waving guns at each other and shouting in French, threatening to kill one another. They had separated and both carried guns in holsters. On one occasion, Luis took a shot at Louisa, and missed her by mere inches. She had him arrested and he'd been convicted and sentenced to 18 months in prison. He was free on appeal bond when his problems really escalated.

One cause of their battles was a young man named John Mitchell who was rumored to have been Louisa's lover (after all, Louisa was known to have been married once before she married Luis, and divorcees were not held in high regard in the late Victorian era). Mitchell lived with the Embertos. Ms. Armijo reported that Mitchell was actually Louisa's son; the product of her earlier marriage. Whatever his status, he also packed a gun.

The matter came to a head on the evening of Saturday, April 30, 1898. Based on Mr. Garcia's narrative, it is difficult to say exactly where the events took place. At one point he indicated that they took place in a nearby residence which Emberto had rented from Manuel Gonzales. At another he indicates the residence of Luis Garcia and at yet a third, the Territorial House itself.

On that evening, Luis told Mr. Garcia's father that he was going to kill Louisa later that same night. The elder Garcia did not believe him, but he did tell Louisa. She didn't believe it, either. In fact, she even took off her own gun and hung it behind a door. But Luis was serious. He showed up later in the evening and when the dogs outside began barking, he shot them, at least shot *at* them. Upon seeing Luis, Louisa ran for her gun, but she was too late. The two of them struggled and Luis fired three times; two bullets struck Louisa, one in the neck. She bled to death.

Mr. Garcia said it was also believed that Luis intended to kill John Mitchell and another man by the name of Ramon Gutierrez. No mention is made of what grudge he held against Gutierrez, but he failed to kill either man. Mitchell was away attending a dance at the Anesito Armijo house and when Luis went to the Gutierrez house, the family kept him out.

The story is a little vague as to where Luis spent the night after the killing, but clearly he spent it drinking. On Sunday morning he tried to get a horse from Francisco Gonzales, presumably to get away. Gonzales could not, or would not, give him one. Luis then barricaded himself in a nearby house, probably the residence of Luis Garcia.

In the meantime, the local judge was notified of what Luis had done. He ordered that several men post themselves where they could watch Emberto's activity. The judge also ordered that Bernalillo County Sheriff Tom Hubbell[4] be summoned. His instructions were that no one was to shoot at Luis until the sheriff could arrive and give orders to do so.

At one point during the day, Luis came out of hiding and asked one of his watchers, Filiberto Gurule, to have a drink with him. Gurule declined and Luis opened fire on the informal posse. No one was hurt, and no one fired back.[5]

53

By the time Sheriff Hubbell arrived, about 40 men, all armed, had gathered around. One of them, according to Mr. Garcia, was a Navajo Indian named Jose de la Cruz who was something of a local marksman. De la Cruz was stationed behind a wall with a clear view of the door where Luis showed himself from time to time. By then, too, Luis Emberto was quite drunk.

Hubbell approached the front door and told Luis that he had come for him. Luis said, "Take me if you're such a big man!" Luis opened fire on the sheriff at close range and missed him completely (Ms. Armijo reported that one of his shots came close enough that it took a button off of the sheriff's coat sleeve). Hubbell ordered de la Cruz to fire, which the Indian did. His bullet struck Luis in the forehead, killing him instantly. Mr. Garcia reported that Hubbell then fired a bullet into Emberto's chest. Hubbell later denied it, but claimed that one of his deputies did so.

Research by Ms. Armijo indicates that Emberto was killed by Hubbell's deputies, and no Navajo marksman was involved. She said that she had heard a version of the story which indicated that an Indian marksman was involved, but he was from Sandia Pueblo, not Navajo. (De la Cruz, she noted, is not a name common to either Sandia or Navajo people.) The official version, she stated, did not mention an Indian marksman.[6]

Thus the matter was concluded. The local priest denied Luis and Louisa burial in the church cemetery and so, according to Mr. Garcia, they were buried about 500 feet behind the Territorial House in unmarked graves.

Luis Emberto, Jr., left Corrales one week after his parents died, for points east. He never returned. Mr. Garcia said he believed that the young man became a professor at Columbia University in New York.

John Mitchell later married, but what became of him is not known.

Tom Hubbell served as Bernalillo County Sheriff until 1905.

ENDNOTES:

[1] For many years the Territorial House was owned by Robert and Cuca Gilliland. Robert died in 1975 and Cuca sold the establishment in 1987. She retained rights to the name and the new owners, Arturo Jaramillo among them, renamed it. It has changed hands in recent years.

[2] For a bit of historical perspective, the building would have been constructed at a time when New Mexico was under the rule of the Spanish king. This would have been during the U. S. presidential administrations of John Adams and Thomas Jefferson.

[3] Bob Gilliland died of a heart attack after being involved in a gunfight at the Territorial House Saloon on October 13, 1974. There is an account of the fight on pages 56-58.

[4] Corrales was in Bernalillo County at the time. Sandoval County was not created until 1903.

[5] Gilliland heard another version of the story in which shots were exchanged for two hours before the sheriff arrived.

[6] Rosie Armijo consulted with Corrales natives about the case, and she also cited news reports in the Albuquerque *Morning Democrat* dated May 3, 1898.

Corrales, Sandoval County
1975

Three Men Shot – Two Die
Saloonkeeper Dies of Heart Attack
Booze Caused the Affray

Not all saloon gunfights took place along the dusty streets of Old West towns. This extremely violent incident took place near the beginning of the fourth quarter of the 20th century in a village along a paved road.

Like many such events, details regarding what led up to the fight are somewhat contradictory, and some of the actual events during the battle are unclear. What is clear is that when the smoke cleared, three men were dead, and one other was seriously wounded.

About noon on Monday, October 13, 1975, two strangers walked into the saloon portion of the Territorial House Restaurant in Corrales, New Mexico. The Sandoval County Sheriff at the time, Bob Budhager, said later that they may have intended to have a meal but instead began drinking. One of them, Richard Kaufman, drank much more than he should have, and engaged in arm wrestling contests with some local men. The competition became less than friendly, with sizable bets being made. Kaufman became sufficiently obnoxious that he was thrown out of the bar. One story goes that he was dragged out the door by bar patrons. He pledged to return to "clean the place out." Kaufman's companion was not identified, and was apparently willing to let the matter go. Kaufman was not.

Kaufman returned to his temporary place of work in Albuquerque at about 8:00 p.m. where his drunkenness was duly noted. Where he spent the time in-between is not known. At around 9:00 p.m. Kaufman returned to the Territorial House Saloon, armed with a *machete*-type knife with a curved blade. Before he could cause any damage with it, he was set upon by the bar's owners, Robert Gilliland and Ernie Monie Sánchez. Local legend holds that Kaufman was injured with his own knife, but news accounts of the day do not indicate so.

As altercation took place, Kaufman's companion, Jerry Lee DeLorenzo — who was not the man who had been with him earlier — entered the bar and assumed a military sort of stance as he yelled, "Freeze!" He aimed a pistol and began firing. He hit Sánchez three times, and may have fatally shot Kaufman. There is some debate about that. DeLorenzo then fled into the parking lot.

Gilliland grabbed a military type M-2 carbine and chased DeLorenzo outside where he began firing at the shooter. DeLorenzo soon went down. Gilliland had served 18 years on the New Mexico State Police and was very familiar with the use of firearms. Gilliland returned to the bar where he took the time to call his wife and tell her about the fight. He assured her that he was alright. He took a seat on a bar stool, and about 45 minutes later he suffered a heart attack and collapsed. Another version is that he was standing when he was stricken and fell into the arms of a deputy sheriff. Yet a third version holds that he was talking with a State Police officer when he collapsed. He was declared dead on arrival at Albuquerque's Presbyterian Hospital. His wife, Cuca, said later that he had no history of heart trouble.

Sánchez was transported to the hospital where he was in critical condition for several days before he finally recovered.

But of course there is more to the story. Since Sánchez had been armed too, with a .38-caliber handgun, and firing; and since Gilliland may have had a .38-caliber handgun in addition to his .30 caliber carbine, and may have fired his pistol, too; and DeLorenzo was blazing away, with a .38-caliber semi-automatic, apparently somewhat at random, it was difficult to determine just who shot whom. This was compounded by the fact that eight 9-millimeter cartridges were found at the scene and no 9-mm gun was ever located. What is certain is that Gilliland shot DeLorenzo at least 22 times, and maybe more. The M-2 carbine carried a 30-round magazine, and legend holds that he emptied it, before he beat DeLorenzo with the stock until he broke it. DeLorenzo's gun was found some 30 feet away from his body, but investigators believe that someone tossed it away from the body after the shooting ended.

No one was arrested as a result of the Territorial House shoot-out since all of the shooters were dead, except for Monie Sánchez, and he was clearly much more a victim than an offender. The restaurant soon resumed operations, run by members of the Gilliland and Sánchez families. Gilliland's wife and sons ultimately operated it until it was sold in 1987, and the name changed. To old timers, though, it will always be the Territorial House.

SOURCES:

Albuquerque *Journal*, October 14, 15, & 24, 1975
Albuquerque *Tribune*, October 14, 15, & 23, 1975
Donnie Chávez, longtime Corrales resident
Jim Henrie, longtime Corrales resident
The Santa Fe *New Mexican*, October 14, 1975

Crossroads, Lea County
1932

Deputy Jim Clifton Dies
After Gunfight with Outlaws
Kills Two Gunmen — Robbery Loot Not Found

Lea County Deputy Sheriff Jim Clifton and a citizen named D. A. Jones sat drinking coffee in Bullard's Cafe in Tatum on the morning of February 24, 1932, when Clifton got a telephone call. The sheriff's office advised the deputy to be on the lookout for two or three men who had just robbed the Dean Hardware Store in Lovington. The robbers were believed to be heading toward Tatum. Only minutes later, Clifton saw a car fitting the description, going north.

Clifton took up pursuit and stopped the car two or three miles south of the community of Crossroads. The deputy got out of his car as two men got out of the suspect car.

"I'd like to talk to you boys," Clifton said.

One of the men, an Oklahoma bank robber named Walter Carlocke, 22, produced a .41-caliber revolver. Clifton was able to take it away from him, but not before the second outlaw, John O'Dell, 23, shot

59

the deputy, several times, with a .38-caliber revolver. Bullets struck the deputy's left shoulder and arm and one took him in the stomach, passing nearly all the way through his body. Bleeding and reeling, Clifton drew his own gun and fired with telling effect. He shot Carlocke once in the heart and O'Dell twice in the chest. Both men died at the scene.

Clifton managed to get back into his car and drive himself to the schoolhouse in Crossroads. A teacher there, seeing how badly wounded the deputy was, drove him to the Crossroads Store where local folks provided what emergency treatment they could[1]. Doctors from Tatum and Lovington rushed to the scene. An airplane from Roswell was ordered but no one bothered to tell the pilot what his chore would be. He showed up in an open cockpit, two-seater, plane. Clifton was moved by automobile to Tatum where a "cabin plane" picked him up about dark that evening for a flight to a hospital in Lubbock, Texas, nearly 100 miles away. Deputy Clifton died at 9:45 p.m.

Medical authorities said that even if Clifton had received comprehensive medical attention from the very beginning, he likely could not have been saved. His wounds were too severe.

Rumors soon abounded that Clifton stopped the wrong men and one newspaper account read:

> Carlocke was wanted in Waurika, Okla., for bank robbery, officers said, and O'Dell was tentatively identified as an escaped convict from the Oklahoma State penitentiary. Neither were implicated in the robbery of the hardware store, officers said, after an investigation.

These allegations were supported by the fact that no loot was found at the scene of the shooting. Some folks believed a third man was involved, and a third gun *was* found in the outlaw's car. Some years later Clifton's sister received information that a convict in the Huntsville, Texas, prison admitted that he was the third man present when Carlocke and O'Dell were killed. He said he remained concealed until Clifton drove away from the scene and then took the loot and hid in some sand hills nearby. He later made his way cross-country, 30 or so miles, to the highway near Elida. He hitched a ride north to Portales and made good his escape.

A sidelight to this story has to do with the fact that Clovis police had received a tip that Carlocke and O'Dell were to meet a third man at a local hotel. They had staked out the place and were waiting for them to arrive when the outlaws were shot and killed near Crossroads. The Clovis officers expected a gunfight with the wanted men. As a newsman wrote at the time, "…fate had a whim."

Folks around Tatum didn't care about questions regarding the dead criminals. An estimated 1,000 people attended Deputy Clifton's funeral.

The Largest Concourse of People
In the History of Town

> Jim Clifton...was a born officer, who knew not fear; a man who has many times looked death in the face without flinching; a man who has been instrumental in making this county a place that is shunned by criminals, and [he] wiped off the books two of the most desperate characters that have ever visited this section....
>
> In his passing, law and order in New Mexico have lost a champion; in his passing a place has been made vacant that cannot be filled, for there was but one Jim Clifton — the mould [sic] in which he was cast has been broken, and the like of him, in these parts, will never be duplicated. We knew him. We liked him. Even those who felt the weight of his authority, respected him, and stood with bowed heads, sorrowing, when they found that his earthly career was over....
>
> It was a terrific blow — a few hours before he was strong and vigorous; a few hours before he smiled, he laughed, then the crashing of heavy pistols, and his race was run.

61

We grieve with the sorrowing wife, we sympathize with the weeping mother, and we bow our head with the grieving father, brothers and sisters.

ENDNOTE:

[1] In another version of the story, it was a local rancher who heard the shots and reached Deputy Clifton first, and who took him to the Crossroads store.

SOURCES:

Albuquerque *Journal*, February 25, 1932

Don Bullis, *New Mexico's Finest: Peace Officers Killed in the Line of Duty, 1847-1999*

Clovis *Evening News-Journal*, February 25, 1932

Lovington *Daily Leader*, May 10, 1990

Santa Fe *New Mexican*, February 25, 1932

Lea County Sheriff's Department

Española, Rio Arriba County
1884

Rancher Romero Killed by Rustlers Near Cabezon
Rustler Castillo Killed, Brother Wounded
Gunfight with Posse at Española

In March of 1884, a gang of outlaws led by brothers Candido and Manuel Castillo rode out of the village of Cebolleta,[1] New Mexico. They rode to the northeast where they intended to steal cattle around the village of Cabezon.[2]

The Castillos were desperate men. A reward of $1,000 was offered for Candido for the shooting of Mariano Larragoite in Colorado in 1879; and both men were wanted for the murder of José Apodaca at Cebolleta in 1883. And these lawless men operated in a lawless land. Cabezon was about 70 miles by trail from Albuquerque, the county seat. Sheriff Perfecto Armijo rarely, if ever, visited the small community and he had no deputy stationed there. The town had no marshal or constable.

Candido and Manuel succeeded in stealing cattle, but a posse of citizens from Cabezon took up pursuit and soon overtook the outlaws. In the gunfight that followed, rancher Juan Romero[3] was killed while the brothers managed to escape. Killing Romero was a serious mistake. Within a very short time, rewards totaling nearly $3,000[4]—an enormous sum at the time—were offered for the brothers. Merchants Rudolph Haberland and William Kanzenbach offered $500. Governor Lionel Shelton offered $500 from the Territorial coffers. José de Baca of Cabezon offered $200 and Romero's widow another $300. The people of the near-by village of Casa Salazar offered additional reward money, as did an Albuquerque resident named Charles Lewis.

Initially, the pursuers of the Castillos had no luck. The country back toward Cibolleta and Mt. Taylor was rugged, with few people and many canyons and arroyos. The trail was lost and the brothers seemed to have disappeared. But $3,000 created a lot of interest. A posse led by Bernalillo County deputy sheriff Jesús Montoya, which included men from Casa Salazar and Cabezon and a Navajo tracker, picked up the trail and followed the brothers northeast, past Santa Fe and on to Española.

Deputy Montoya and his posse set a trap at Amado Lucero's store in Española, and the Castillos rode into it. When the shooting was over, both of the outlaws were wounded and their horses killed. Manuel died later that day and Candido escaped.[5]

Candido, at least temporarily, joined another outlaw band in or near the town of Abiquiú, north of Española. He moved on to Colorado, but his freedom was short-lived. He was captured near Walsenburg the following year and returned to Albuquerque. Tried and convicted of second-degree murder, he received a sentence of five years in prison. Upon completion of his jail term in July 1890, he returned to Colorado. In 1891, he participated in the killings of two men at Red Hill Pass. The sheriff of Park County, Colorado shot and killed the outlaw near his cabin later the same year.

Thus did the long arm of the law reach out to both the Castillo brothers.

Cabezon,[6] where this little drama began, is today a ghost town. At times in the past it was estimated to have had a population of 300 to 400 served by several mercantile establishments and saloons. It was also a main stop on the stagecoach line from Santa Fe to Fort Wingate, near Gallup. There was a large population of Navajo Indians in the area during the town's early life.

Located near the banks of the Rio Puerco, Cabezon was named for a 2,200 foot tall volcanic plug located nearby. Sources vary as to exactly when the community was first settled. Church records show that Francisco Montoya and Juliana Montes Vigil were married at El Puesto del Cerro Cabezon on March 19, 1772. T. M. Pearce in *New Mexico Place Names* indicates that Juan Maestas first settled the town in 1826. James and Barbara Sherman in *Ghost Towns and Mining Camps of New Mexico* report that the town was settled in the 1870s.

The earliest settlers who arrived in the area were all subjects of the Spanish Crown. They were members of the Montoya, Vigil, Gonzales and Baca families. Later ranchers also had familiar names: Sandoval, Leyba, Chávez, Valencia and others. The Anglo traders arrived in the years after the Civil War. Haberland and Kanzenbach were mentioned above. Others included Oliver Perry Hovey, John Pflueger, Charles Holman and Richard Heller. Heller operated a store in Cabezon from 1889 until his death in 1947. His wife continued to run the business until the town itself died in 1950.

And what caused the demise of Cabezon? The specifics vary, but in general the town became a victim of the changing times. The coming of the railroad meant the end of the stagecoach lines.[7] Navajo Indians, once a major factor in the local economy, moved further west and no longer traded in Cabezon. Land around the community became severely overgrazed, and ranching profits fell. The Great Depression came in the 1930s and residents left town to seek employment elsewhere. The Rio Puerco became a trickle and efforts to dam it were not successful. Paved roads (State Road 44, now U. S. Route 550, was paved in 1934) and automobiles meant that shopping—with greater selection and lower prices—could be done in larger communities. In the final analysis, there just ceased to be a reason for the continued existence of Cabezon. The town could, and did, fight back against the likes of the Castillo brothers, but it could not protect itself from the encroachment of time.

NOTE: What remains of Cabezon today is located on private property, and those who own it do not allow visitors, and for good reason: Many buildings and the cemetery have been severely vandalized. Readers who wish to know what Cabezon looked like should check out a 1973 movie called *My Name is Nobody* starring Henry Fonda. Part of it was filmed there.

ENDNOTES:

[1] *Cebolleta* has been corrupted into the modern spelling, *Seboyeta*: "a place prolific with onions," according to T. M. Pierce in *New Mexico Place Names.*

[2] *Cabezon* means "big head." The town was in Bernalillo County in 1884, but has been in Sandoval County since 1903.

[3] One source reports that Juan Romero was a deputy sheriff, but no corroboration has been found.

[4] At a time when a cowboy earned about $30 per month, the reward amounted to more than eight years of pay.

[5] One source says that it was Candido who was killed in Española, and Manuel who escaped.

[6] The town at various times has been called *Porteria, La Puesta, La Posta,* and *Cerro de la Cabeza.* Oliver Perry Hovey was instrumental in changing the name to Cabezon in 1891.

[7] The Santa Fe to Wingate stagecoach line lasted longer than most. It did not cease operations until 1912.

Fort Stanton, Lincoln County
1862

Captain Graydon & Doctor Whitlock
In Gun Duel on Stanton Parade Ground — Both Killed
Colonel Carson Outraged, Threatens Arrests

Never heard of Paddy Graydon? Not many have, in spite of the fact that James "Paddy" Graydon was one of New Mexico's most interesting characters, known to many as the Desert Tiger.

A bit of confusion about his date of birth, to begin with. One source indicates that he was born in 1832, while another reports he first saw the light of day in 1842. The latter date seems a bit unlikely since he would only have been 20 years old when he died.

Graydon was born in Northern Ireland but made his way to the United States, and the Southwest, as a young man. He enlisted in the United State Army's 1st Dragoons in April 1853. He marched west and was assigned to Company G, stationed at Los Lunas, New Mexico, under the command of Captain Richard Stoddart Ewell, a well-know Indian fighter of the day. Graydon participated in a number of forays into the Mescalero Apache homeland, and was present when Captain

Henry Whiting Stanton was killed near El Rio Peñasco in January 1855. Fort Stanton, near Lincoln, was of course named for him.

In 1856, Graydon's unit was assigned to what would become Arizona. He left the Army in 1858 and opened a hotel about four miles south of Fort Buchanan. It came to be called the Casa Blanca (for obvious reasons), and it was one of the toughest saloons on the New Mexico frontier (remember that President Lincoln didn't separate Arizona and New Mexico until 1863). Tough or not, it seems to have been successful. One source reports that Graydon had assets valued at $13,000 in 1860, a considerable amount of money at the time.

In 1861, Graydon participated in the celebrated Bascom Affair in which Apaches, under Cochise, killed six white captives and in return six Apache hostages were hanged by a U. S. Army detachment under Lt. George Bascom. The latter event sparked a war which lasted 10, or so, years.

By late in 1861, with the coming of the United States Civil War to New Mexico, Governor Henry Connelly commissioned Graydon, a staunch Union supporter, as a Captain and the commander of an "Independent Spy Company." Graydon and his men were mighty good at what they did. One Confederate soldier complained that Graydon (he called him O'Graden) "…knew every move we made" before the Battle of Valverde (February 21, 1862). Maybe, but the Confederates still managed a victory in that battle.

It was Graydon who suggested that Union troops load two old mules with explosives, light the fuses, and then drive them into the Confederate camp. The plan failed when the animals refused to commit suicide for the Union cause, although they were both killed anyway. Graydon was a conspicuous participant in the Valverde battle.

In October of the same year, Graydon and his troop rode to Gallinas Springs in what is now Lincoln County, and initially met peacefully with Manuelito, a Mescalero Apache Chief, who was there because Colonel Kit Carson had directed him to be. Later, however, near Cement Springs, three miles from Gallinas Springs, Graydon and Manuelio met again. Graydon killed Manuelito; and nearly a dozen other

Apaches were killed by troops under Graydon's command. In early November, 1862, Dr. John M. Whitlock (one source reports that his first name was James), an army surgeon in Kit Carson's First New Mexico Volunteers, accused Graydon of murdering Manuelito and the other Apaches. On the afternoon of November 4, the two men met in the sutler's store at Fort Stanton and exchanged accusations and insults, but no blood was

Chief Manuelito

shed. On the following morning, though, on the fort's parade ground, the lead began to fly. Whitlock, slightly wounded in the wrist, killed Captain Graydon (actually shot him in the chest and he died four days later). In retaliation, Graydon's men murdered Whitlock. One report indicated that the *medico* was shot more than 100 times, but others indicate that his body contained but 20 bullet wounds, plus damage done by a shotgun.

Carson was so angry at the murder of Dr. Whitlock that he threatened to hang the entire detachment. In the end, though, only three were charged with the crime. The three were arrested and removed to Santa Fe to await trial. They all escaped, but were eventually recaptured. They were scheduled to go on trial in February 1863, but for an unknown reason, the court was adjourned, and if there was a final adjudication of the matter, the record has not been found.

Graydon is mentioned by a number of historians, several of them listed below; but the best treatment of his life is Jerry Thompson's book, *Captain Paddy Graydon: Desert Tiger*.

OTHER SOURCES:

Don Alberts, *Rebels on the Rio Grande*

Mrs. B. C. Hernandez, "Death of J. M. Whitlock," *New Mexico Historical Review*, January 1941

Jacqueline Dorgan Meketa, *Legacy of Honor*

Richard Melzer, *Buried Treasures*

Rathbun & Alexander, *New Mexico Frontier Military Place Names*

Hampton Sides, *Blood and Thunder*

Dan Thrapp, *Encyclopedia of Frontier Biography*

Fort Sumner & Taiban, DeBaca County
1880

Outlaws Bowdre & O'Folliard Shot, Killed
By Sheriff Garrett's Posse
Billy the Kid Captured Uninjured

Everyone who has been in New Mexico for more than fifteen minutes knows about Billy the Kid (William H. Bonney); knows that Pat Garrett killed him on July 14, 1881 at Fort Sumner, where he was buried alongside two of his cohorts under a tombstone that reads, "PALS." Not many folks, though, know who those "pals" were. Fame for Charlie Bowdre and Tom O'Folliard did not survive their deaths, in the way that Billy's did.

In many ways, Charlie Bowdre was an unlikely partner for Bonney. For one thing, Bowdre was more than 10 years older than Bonney, born in 1848 in Mississippi. Many historians agree that Billy was born in New York City, probably in 1859. Bowdre drifted around the West as a young man, and is known to have spent some time in Dodge City, Kansas and Fort Griffin, Texas, before he arrived in New Mexico in the company of Josiah "Doc" Scurlock around 1875. Scurlock would also

71

Charlie Bowdre

become a cohort of Billy the Kid. Around the same time Bowdre married Manuela Herrera and purchased a farm on the Rio Ruidoso in Lincoln County.

His farming days didn't last long, even though some who have written of him indicate that he preferred farming as a way of life. By 1878 he was managing a ranch northeast of Fort Sumner where he became acquainted with Billy Bonney, Tom O'Folliard and others of the same ilk. The three of them became fast friends.

Bowdre was involved in some of the most stirring events of the Lincoln County War including the early fight at Blazer's Mill in April 1878. He was one of an estimated 14 outlaws (or possemen, depending on point of view) that was set upon by Andrew "Buckshot" Roberts. Some say that Roberts was after the bounty on some of the outlaws, while others believe that he stumbled upon the gang accidentally (which certainly makes the most sense). Roberts was able to wound two or three of the outlaws before he was himself shot. Bowdre often gets credit for shooting Roberts, but Billy Bonney also claimed credit. After the wounded Roberts took cover, he shot and killed Dick Brewer — who many described as the leader of the group. That ended the fight. Roberts died the next day and he and Brewer were buried side by side on a hill near Blazer's Mill.

The Five Days' Battle in Lincoln took place the following July, and Bowdre was there, too. Some say, in fact, that he held a leadership position. He escaped from that melee alive; and while he remained with Bonney over the next few years, he made a couple of tentative efforts at making peace, none of which succeeded. He was present at Fort Sumner on December 19, 1880 when a posse led by Sheriff Pat Garrett ambushed the gang and killed Tom O'Folliard.

His own death was to come only two days later when Garrett's posse surrounded a stone shack at Stinking Springs, near present-day Taiban in eastern New Mexico. When Bowdre stepped outside just after sunrise to feed his horse, the posse opened fire and he was mortally wounded. He is said to have opened his arms toward the posse and to have said, "I wish, I wish…" before he died. Many credit Pat Garrett with killing Bowdre, but there is no proof that he fired the fatal shot. Garrett paid for the suit in which Bowdre was buried.

This photograph is proported to be Billy the Kid being captured at Stinking Springs, December 21, 1880. Owner of photograph says Pat Garrett is at extreme left and Bob Olinger is next to him. Billy is on the extreme right where a deputy aims a Colt revolver at Billy's head. Charlie Bowdre was killed in the encounter at Stinking Springs. Billy the Kid was ambushed by Sheriff Garrett and his posse on December 19, 1880, in Fort Sumner. Photograph has not been authenticated. Photograph courtesy a private collector, England.

Tom O'Folliard

Tom O'Folliard was born near Uvalde, Texas, and was very close to Billy Bonney in age. He was orphaned as a youngster and raised by a Mexican family at Monclave in the state of Coahuila, Mexico. He arrived in Lincoln County in the spring of 1878, in time to get tangled up in the Lincoln County War. He, too, was present at the Five Days' Battle, and survived it, although he was wounded in the shoulder as he fled.

Tom also stayed with Bonney in the intervening years before Pat Garrett was elected Sheriff of Lincoln County. On December 19, 1880, Garrett's posse holed-up in Fort Sumner in the hope that Bonney and his bunch would ride in, and they did just that. O'Folliard rode in the front with another outlaw named Tom Pickett when Garrett ordered them to halt. O'Folliard reached for his pistol as two or three of the possemen opened fire with rifles. A bullet took him in the chest, near the heart. He tried to flee along with the others, but could not.

He remained alive as Garrett and some others carried him inside, out of the cold, and laid him out on the floor.

"Oh my God," he cried, "is it possible I must die?"

"Tom, your time is short," Garrett replied.

"The sooner the better. I will be out of pain." O'Folliard died soon after saying it.

Billy Bonney would be dead, too, less than seven months later, also at the hand of Pat Garrett.

Readers who choose to visit the "PALS" tombstone in the old military cemetery at Fort Sumner should not suppose as they look at it that the bones of the three outlaws rest beneath it. A flood washed away the grave markers more than 100 years ago. No one knows exactly where in the cemetery the bodies repose, and there are some that don't believe that Billy's body is there at all.

SOURCES:

Burns, Walter Noble, *The Saga of Billy the Kid*
Fulton, Maurice G., *History of the Lincoln County War*
Keleher, William A., *Violence in Lincoln County*
Wallis, Michael, *Billy the Kid: The Endless Ride*
(Note: There are numerous books available on Billy the Kid and the Lincoln County War.)

Socorro County Sheriff Elfego Baca

Frisco Plaza, Catron County
1884

*People in Western New Mexico Town
Harassed by Texas Cowboys
Deputy Baca Takes Action: Two Killed*

The saga of Elfego Baca, gunfighter, began in November of 1884. He was 19 years old at the time and a resident of Socorro, New Mexico. He decided that he wanted to be a lawman, a deputy sheriff in particular, but the sheriff would not give him an appointment. Elfego solved that problem by simply buying his own badge from a mail-order house. When he learned that Texas cowboys were in the habit of hoorawing a small town in western Socorro County, he pinned on his badge, armed himself, and rode off to put a stop to it.

Upper San Francisco Plaza[1] was located about 130 miles west of Socorro. It was a quiet town of little note until several Texas cattle outfits began grazing large herds in the area. The original inhabitants of the village were almost entirely Hispanic and the Texas drovers were almost entirely Anglo. The latter group found entertainment in getting drunk and shooting up the town and generally terrorizing the native

77

population. On one occasion the cowboys tied a young boy named Martínez to a tree and used him for target practice. He was wounded four times, but survived.

Little, it seemed, could be done to stop the disorder because the Texans were better armed than the natives and they clearly demonstrated their willingness to disregard the law. A local justice of the peace had once bothered to jail one of the cowboys for disturbing the peace; only to be set upon by a band of rowdies and sent scurrying with gunshots at his heels. The cowboys then broke down the jail door and released their friend.

On the same day that young Elfego arrived in town, so did a cowboy named McCarty[2]. McCarty went to work at getting drunk in Milligan's saloon, and then shooting up the village. He rode up and down the street taking potshots at anything or anyone he chose. Baca went to the justice of the peace and demanded an arrest warrant for the miscreant; but the judge refused, saying he feared more harm would befall the town in trying to stop the cowboy than if they just let the matter pass. Elfego would have none of that. He was a peace officer, he announced, and he would do his duty.

He did. He found McCarty standing in the street visiting with some of his friends. The self-appointed deputy grabbed the cowboy by the collar, shoved the barrel of his pistol into the drover's ear and ordered him to hotfoot it for the jail. McCarty complied and no one interfered.

Late in the afternoon a bunch of cowboys made an effort to free their friend. Baca appeared at the door, gun in hand. He gave the drovers until the count of three to get out of town. He quickly made the count and opened fire. One shot hit a cowboy in the knee and the noise of the gunshots spooked a horse ridden by the ranch foreman, a man named Perham, who was killed when the animal fell on top of him. The Texans retreated.

Word of the shooting, and the death of Perham, spread quickly and soon a large number of cowboys assembled in Frisco Plaza. Fearing the worst, a group of citizens, led by a man named J. H. Cook, arranged a truce. Baca agreed to deliver McCarty to the Justice of the Peace who by then had agreed to hear the case. The cowboy was fined five dollars and released.

Baca prepared to leave town, but it was the Texans' turn to take aggressive action. A shot was fired and Elfego retreated down an alley and, after evicting a woman and two small children, took cover in a small, flimsy, one-room house of a type called a *jacal*[3]. Under the leadership of a Texas man named Jim Herne, an attack was soon made. Herne held the residents of Frisco Plaza in utter contempt, and often said so in certain and blasphemous terms. He demanded that Baca leave his shelter, and Elfego's response was two well-placed shots into the cowboy's body. He fell dead on the spot. It was nine o'clock in the morning.

The Texans took cover nearby and put a steady barrage of gunfire into the hut. They kept it up all day, firing hundreds of rounds of ammunition. Baca returned fire from time to time, but no one was hit. None of the Texans attempted to approach and Elfego was unscathed.

The floor in a *jacal* is about 18 inches lower than the ground around it, so the deputy had protection from the bullets. By late afternoon the cowboys had fired enough lead into the house that one wall collapsed. Around midnight, they used dynamite to try and dislodge Baca, and part of the roof and another wall collapsed.

The Texans hoped they had killed Baca with the dynamite, but they learned better on the morning of the second day when they smelled food cooking. Elfego had managed to make a fire in the stove and prepare his breakfast. At midmorning, a cowboy attempted to approach by hiding behind the front part of a cast-iron stove. Baca watched and waited for an opportunity, which the cowboy provided when he peeked above his armor. Elfego split his scalp with a single shot. The cowboy did not die[4].

Late in the afternoon of the second day, a deputy sheriff named Ross and J. H. Cook, with the help of Francisquito Naranjo, convinced Baca to surrender. They agreed to protect him from the Texans as he was taken to Socorro to face charges for killing Herne. Elfego agreed provided that he did not have to give up his guns until he reached

Socorro, and that he be allowed to ride backwards on the buckboard so that he could not be taken by surprise. Ross and Baca left town that same evening.

Thus ended the gunfight at Upper Frisco Plaza, and thus began the legend of Elfego Baca. An estimated 4,000 rounds of ammunition were fired into the *jacal* by an estimated 80 Texans[5] during a period of 36 hours. Eight bullets had hit a broom handle inside. Every spoon, fork and knife was struck by at least one bullet. About 370 bullets penetrated the door. The only thing in the shack not hit, besides Elfego, was a plaster statue of *Mi Señora Santa Ana*.

Elfego was jailed for four months and tried twice for the killings at Upper Frisco Plaza. He was acquitted both times.

This was only the beginning of a long and adventurous life. Baca died in 1945 at the age of 80.

ENDNOTES:

[1] Also known as Milligan's Plaza, after a local saloon keeper, now called Reserve, it is the seat of Catron County.

[2] Not to be confused with William McCarty, aka Billy the Kid.

[3] A *jacal* is not much more than a shack. It is constructed of vertical sticks — some writers generously call them posts — chinked with adobe mud.

[4] Some legends hold that three or four Texans were killed at Upper Frisco Plaza, but it is more likely that Herne was the only one shot to death while several were wounded.

[5] Eighty is the generally accepted number. Marc Simmons in *Albuquerque, A Narrative History* indicates the number was "several dozen".

SOURCES:

Howard Bryan, *Incredible Elfego Baca*

Kyle S. Crichton, *Law and Order, Ltd. The Rousing Life of Elfego Baca of New Mexico*

Stan Sager, *¡Viva Elfego! The Case for Elfego Baca, Hispanic Hero*

Gallup, McKinley County
1935

Sheriff Carmichael and One Killed,
Seven Wounded as Unemployed Riot
(Headline, Gallup Independent, *April 4, 1935)*

Things were tough in the United States in 1935. The Great Depression was firmly in place, unemployment was high and money was scarce. Banks foundered or failed. The drought, and resulting Dust Bowl, worsened monthly. Farms and ranches failed. Manufacturing declined and mines of all kinds closed. Distrust, agitation and violence were the unfortunate results.

Gallup, New Mexico, found itself in the maelstrom of the times.

Coal mining was a significant factor in the Gallup economy. So important was it that the community of Gamerco, located a couple of miles north of town, was named for the Gallup American Coal Company. By the middle 1930s, with the demand for coal down, many miners found themselves out of work.

Many of them lived in company housing at a place called Chihuahuita. In 1934 a local state senator named C. F. Vogel bought the settle-

81

ment from Gamerco. At the time it consisted of about 100 houses, many of them occupied by unemployed miners. Vogel offered those living there an opportunity to either begin paying rent, or to purchase their respective homes on the installment plan. Most refused, and they were supported by the National Miners Union[1], the International Labor Defense organization, and the Community Party's Unemployed Union.

Vogel took legal action in early 1935 to enforce his ownership prerogatives and Justice of the Peace William J. Bickel soon issued eviction orders against the squatters. One of those evicted was Victor Campos, whose house was boarded up by officers after the order was carried out.

It didn't stay boarded up for very long. Campos, along with Ezquio Navarro, Jennie Lovato and a "mob" of about 50 other miners tore the boards off and moved Campos' belongings back into the house. All three were promptly arrested on a complaint signed by Vogel. Mrs. Lovato was released on her own recognizance, but the men were jailed pending a court appearance scheduled for the morning of April 4.

Sheriff Mack Carmichael did not take the matter lightly. Along with Undersheriff Dee Roberts and deputies Edison "Bobcat" Wilson, 27, and Hoy Boggess, 41, he had no problem in getting the prisoners to Bickel's courtroom. A crowd began to gather outside as the proceedings got underway inside. Bickel took no action but continued the case until the following day to allow Navarro time to secure the services of legal counsel. Carmichael decided that rather than risk taking his prisoners through the crowd, he'd take them out the back way; through the judge's chambers, down an alley from Third Street to Second Street and to the jail. The mob—75 to 300 strong, depending on who told the story—learned of the maneuver and thought the suspects had been railroaded and were being returned to jail.[2] The crowd confronted the sheriff on Third Street and demanded the release of Campos and Navarro.

No one knows for sure who fired first. Some believe it was either Ignacio Valarde or Solomon Esquibel. It is known that Sheriff Carmichael was the first to fall, shot in the left arm and just below the right eye; dead on the ground before he drew his own gun. Dee Roberts pulled his gun but could not make the trigger work. He fanned the hammer with the heel of his hand and managed to kill Valarde and seriously wound Esquibel, who died eight days later.

Gunfire continued on both sides. Bobcat Wilson was hit in the chest and rioters Doroteo Andrade, Juan Castro and Pete Moreno were also wounded, along with innocent bystander Mrs. Solidad Sánchez.

Deputy Boggess was beaten about the head with clubs and stabbed in the chest with an ice pick.

Gallup Police Chief Kelsey Pressley and his officers moved into the area and helped break up the mob. Campos and Navarro managed to escape as the crowd scattered. Wounded rioters were taken to St. Mary's hospital in Gallup and wounded officers were taken to Rehoboth Mission hospital. They all survived. In fact, Hoy Boggess, with five stitches and his head swathed in a bandage, rejoined the posse that same evening.

Dee Roberts had previously served as McKinley County sheriff and within minutes of Carmichael's death, he was again elevated to that position. He immediately mobilized a posse of about 100 special deputies that included all the able-bodied members of the American Legion and the Veterans of Foreign Wars, and other citizens. By noon, Gallup was an armed camp. By 2:30 that afternoon, 30 suspects were in custody. By nightfall, the number had reached about 100. The sheriff's goal was to arrest everyone in McKinley County connected with the "radical movement", and in those days that meant Communists and Communist sympathizers.

Later the same day, New Mexico Governor Clyde Tingley ordered E. A. House, chief of the New Mexico State Police,[3] and twelve officers to Gallup. The governor also made the state penitentiary available to confine those arrested and a special railroad car was assigned to take them to Santa Fe. Tingley declined to mobilize the National Guard.

When the dust settled 10 days later, about 150 people had been arrested; 47 of them, including 11 women, charged with murder. The murder charges were possible because of a state statute which provided that all participants in illegal mob activity could be so charged in the event that a peace officer was killed as a result of that activity. 10 of the suspects were bound over for trial after a preliminary hearing.

Trial of the 10 took place in Aztec on a change of venue in October 1935. On the 17th, three of the defendants, Juan Ochoa, Manuel Avitia and Leandro Valarde (the brother of Ignacio Velarde) were convicted of second-degree murder for the death of Mack Carmichael. Judge James McGhee sentenced them to not less than 45, nor more than 60, years in prison. The remaining seven were convicted of rioting. Two of them, Joe Bartol and Willie Gonzales, both American citizens, were ordered to leave New Mexico. The other five, Mexican citizens, were deported to their native country.

The convictions were, of course, appealed. The state Supreme Court reversed Velarde's conviction. Ochoa and Avitia served short prison terms before they were pardoned and set free.

Thus it ended, one of the darker chapters in New Mexico history.

ENDNOTES:

[1] The National Miners Union should not be confused with the United Mine Workers of America. The United Mine Workers cooperated with Gallup authorities after the riot and cancelled local meetings until order was restored.

[2] Bickel was sometimes referred to as "Bail-less" Bickel, according to Erna Fergusson.

[3] The New Mexico State Police was created by the Legislature on February 25, 1935.

SOURCES:

Albuquerque *Journal*, April 4 & 6, 1935

Don Bullis, *New Mexico's Finest: Peace Officers Killed in the Line of Duty, 1847-1999*

Gallup *Independent & Evening Herald*, April 4, 5, 15 & 17, 1935

Erna Fergusson, *Murder & Mystery in New Mexico*

Cpl. Sam Gomez, Gallup correspondence, May, 1989

New Mexico State Police Yearbook, Anniversary 1935-1995

Greathouse Ranch, Lincoln County
1880

Billy the Kid Gang Shoots Up Town
Kills Deputy Jimmy Carlysle at Rural Tavern
White Oaks Posse Burns Road Ranch to the Ground

James Bermuda Carlyle is not a name that springs to mind when one is reminded of the famous gunfights/gunfighters of the Old West. He didn't live long enough to acquire much of a reputation, but those who bother themselves with the esoterica of the late 19th century American Frontier know his name.

Carlyle is believed to have been born in Trumbull County, Ohio, around 1861. He left home at a young age and by the time he reached his middle teens he was working on the buffalo hunting ranges of West Texas. In the summer of 1874 he participated in the second battle at the Adobe Walls in which thirty men — famed lawman Bat Masterson among them — and one woman, held off a thousand Comanche, Kiowa and Cheyenne Indians. Carlyle's name appears on the monument there as Bermuda Carlile.

The route he took is not known, but by November of 1880 Jim Carlyle

Dirty Dave Rudabaugh

was living in the thriving mining town of White Oaks, New Mexico, and working as a blacksmith. That was in the waning days of the famed Lincoln County War. William Bonney (Billy the Kid) remained free, making a general nuisance of himself, and Patrick F. Garrett had just been elected sheriff of Lincoln County on the campaign promise that he would bring a halt to Bonney's criminal career.

Bonney, along with Billy Wilson and Dave Rudabaugh, and perhaps others, stole a herd of horses and drove them into White Oaks on November 28. The nuances of ownership of the animals could be overlooked as a result of great demand for mounts. But a local deputy sheriff named Will Hudgin became suspicious and took up the trail of the outlaws. In the gunfight that followed, Bonney and Wilson both had their horses shot from under them and they were obliged to run for their lives. The outlaws got back into White Oaks on November 30, and for no very good reason Bonney, or one of his toadies, took a shot at another deputy sheriff named James Redman on White Oak's main street.

Jimmy Carlyle, who also served as a Lincoln County deputy sheriff,[1] took a leadership position in the 12-man posse that pursued the miscreants. The chase ended about 40 miles to the north at the Greathouse and Kuch ranch on the White Oaks-Las Vegas Road, near the present-day town of Corona. The ranch house, sometimes called Greathouse Tavern, was actually a saloon and way-station for travelers. The outlaws had the better of the situation as a standoff developed with them inside where it was warm and the posse outside in the cold. Snow covered the ground and the temperature stood at below freezing.

A Greathouse and Kuch employee named Joe Steck became an intermediary between the two groups. It was agreed that "Whiskey Jim" Greathouse—who acquired his nickname by illegally selling liquor to Indians—would join the posse as a hostage if a representative of the law would enter the saloon and discuss the situation with William Bonney.[2] Carlyle agreed and traded places with Greathouse. By late evening the deputy had not returned and the other possemen became concerned. They sent a note into the house saying that if Carlyle was not promptly released, they would shoot Greathouse. Shortly afterward, a shot was heard from outside and what happened next has been the source of debate from that day to this.

One theory is that Carlyle heard the shot and, thinking his posse had killed Greathouse, he dived out a window to save his own life, only to be shot to death by Bonney and the outlaws. Bonney's version of events agreed that Carlyle jumped out the window after the first shot was fired; but Bonney claimed the deputy was actually shot and killed by members of his own posse who, not recognizing him, thought he was attacking them.

The posse withdrew after Carlyle was shot, leaving his body where it fell in the snow. Less than an hour later, the outlaws also fled the scene. Carlyle's body was frozen stiff when Joe Steck found it at daybreak. Another White Oaks posse, this one led by Will Hudgin, burned the road ranch to the ground the following day.

It is not known who fired the shot that created the circumstances leading to Deputy Carlyle's death. Jim Greathouse was arrested in March 1881, and charged as an accessory to the murder of Jim Carlyle. He was released on bond two days later. In December 1881, after rustling some 40 head of cattle from Joel Fowler of Socorro, Fowler shot Greathouse to death in the San Mateo Mountains, west of Socorro.

Lincoln County Sheriff Pat Garrett killed William H. Bonney at Fort Sumner on July 14, 1881. Dave Rudabaugh was killed in Mexico in 1886.

Billy Wilson was later convicted of counterfeiting, and sentenced to

Leavenworth Prison in Kansas, from which he escaped. President Grover Cleveland pardoned him in 1896 at the behest of Pat Garrett. One source says he later became sheriff of Terrell County, Texas. A drunken cowboy killed him there in 1911. Most important is that Wilson was born in 1861 in Trumbull County, Ohio. One source says that Carlyle and Wilson attended school together. That may explain why Carlyle was willing to go into the ranch house/tavern in the first place. But whatever the reason, the result was that Jim Carlyle's career on the Western Frontier ended before he ever reached his 21st birthday.

ENDNOTES:

[1] Historian Don Cline, who spent many years researching Billy the Kid and the Lincoln County War, said that these law officers may not have been deputy sheriffs, but deputies of the White Oaks town marshal. It is certainly unlikely that all members of the posse were sworn deputies.

[2] Cline believes that Kuch was the hostage, and not Greathouse.

SOURCES:

Howard Bryan, *Robbers, Rogues and Ruffians, True Tales of the Wild West*
Don Cline, correspondence, June 1990
H. B. Henning, Ed., *George Curry, 1861-1947, An Autobiography*
William A. Keleher, *Violence in Lincoln County, 1869-1881*
Leon Claire Metz, *The Shooters*
Jay Robert Nash, *Encyclopedia of Western Lawmen & Outlaws*. (This source incorrectly identifies Terrell County as being in New Mexico.)
Dan L. Thrapp, *Encyclopedia of Frontier Biography*, University of Nebraska Press

Hobbs, Lea County
1951

Parks Brothers Go on Shooting Spree
Officer Butler Killed & Clerk Grantham Shot
Killers — High on Drugs — Captured

At age 68, Bob Butler served the Hobbs Police Department as parking control officer. At about 3:30 on Saturday afternoon, July 7, 1951, while making his rounds, Officer Butler stopped to talk with Phil Verner, owner of the K. C. Store on Broadway, and store clerk Ira Grantham.

In the meantime, brothers Speight Fondron Parks, 27, and Gene Afton Parks, 22, entered the Midwest Drug Store down the street and demanded a "redbird" (seconal). The druggist, Robert Prather, said later that he had never heard of anything like that, but thought they wanted some kind of dope. He ordered them out of his store, and they left. The brothers were also reported to have spent some time in an area saloon that day, and other witnesses reported that the Parks brothers appeared to be drunk as they bumped and jostled people while they walked along the busy street.

As they neared the K. C. Store, Officer Butler approached them and when he took Gene by the arm, Speight hit the elderly officer with his fist and knocked him to the pavement. In the fight that followed, Officer Butler was knocked down a total of three times. At struggle's end, Speight Parks removed Butler's service revolver from its holster.

Butler and Grantham fled into the store. Speight Parks pursued them and began firing. Butler was shot first, three times, and fell dead a few feet inside the door and Grantham, 63, also shot three times, died further inside the store. Verner had entered the store first and called the police station for help when the fight between Butler and Parks began.

The Parks brothers fled back into the street. Hobbs policeman R. C. "Pinky" Hamlin captured Gene Parks almost immediately, but Speight managed to hijack a late-model Ford and flee. He wrecked the car and stole a second one from a Hobbs gas station. In all, he stole, and wrecked, four cars and was in the process of stealing a fifth, when Lea County Sheriff's Deputy Bruce McCallum and Hobbs Police Chief Ivan Reed accosted him. McCallum was armed with a 12-gauge pump shotgun.

"Raise your hands, Parks, and raise them empty!" the deputy shouted.

Parks did not respond, and McCallum repeated the order. Then Parks started to take aim with Butler's pistol and McCallum fired. A load of 00 buckshot hit the killer in the right arm and chest. He survived his injury. Feelings in Hobbs ran so high that officers were obliged to move the brothers to the Roswell jail for their own safety.

State Police officer Joe Aven asked Gene Parks if they meant to kill Butler.

"You're damned right we did. I'm glad the old S. O. B. is dead," Parks responded. Speight Parks, an ex-convict, also commented that he had always been curious about the electric chair. "Now it looks like I'll ride out on Old Sparky," he said, meaning the electric chair.

But that wasn't to be. Both brothers were charged with first-degree murder, and at trial, Speight was convicted and sentenced to two life terms in prison. Gene was acquitted.

Speight was stabbed to death by another prisoner, Alejandro Garcia, a convicted car thief, about six months after he reached prison. Garcia was charged with voluntary manslaughter.

SOURCES:

Albuquerque *Tribune*, July 9, 1951
Hobbs *Daily Flare*, July 10, 1951
Hobbs *Daily News-Sun*, July 8, 1951
Hobbs Police Department
Santa Fe *New Mexican*, July 8, 1951
Molly Dunaway (Officer Butler's daughter), 1990

Hope, Eddy County
1922

Texas Outlaw Will-O-Wisp Shoots
Kills New Mexico Lawman
Shot Dead for His Trouble

In early June of 1922, word reached Eddy County Sheriff George Washington Batton that a Texas outlaw called the Longhorn Will-O-Wisp (Pedro Galindo) and two women were hiding at a house—some said a shack—in the town of Hope, about 20 miles west of Artesia in the far northwest corner of the county. Galindo had escaped from the Huntsville, Texas, prison while serving a life sentence for murder.

Batton, along with his deputies and a posse of local cowboys and citizens, surrounded the place. The sheriff wanted to smoke out the occupants, but there was a fear that a fire might be started which would spread. Batton then ordered those inside to surrender, and two women emerged. They said no one else remained inside.

Sheriff Batton approached and entered the front door and one of his deputies, Stone Wilburn, approached the back door. They found the Will-O-Wisp hiding under some clothing behind a dresser. He opened fire on the officers immediately. A soft-nosed bullet bounced off Wilburn's rib and the sheriff took a bullet in the bowel near hip level. Batton and Wilburn opened fire in a rapid succession of shots. The lights inside were blown out then and the firing stopped. As Wilburn staggered outside, the women tried to escape from the scene, only to be caught and held by a couple of the cowboy possemen. Deputies then forced the younger woman to go back into the house. She crawled in on her hands and knees and soon returned with Galindo's gun, a .44-caliber semi-automatic. She said that both men inside the house were dead.

She was right. The posse found Sheriff Batton on the floor. The outlaw was in a corner, shot through the neck and heart. Deputy Wilburn recovered from his wound.

George Batton, 58, had previously served as a deputy sheriff of Brown County in central Texas, where he shot and killed a drunken blacksmith, George Yarber, who had shot and killed Brown County Sheriff Charles Bell on March 23, 1898. Batton then served as Brown County sheriff (1898-1900).

After he arrived in New Mexico, Batton served as Artesia town marshal and Eddy County deputy under sheriffs John M. Hewitt and M. E. Steward before he was elected sheriff in 1920. Batton's son Sam succeeded him as sheriff. Reports at the time indicated that Sam was present at the gunfight that claimed his father's life, but his involvement is not known.

Sources:

Albuquerque *Morning Journal*, June 5, 1922
Carlsbad *Current*, June 9, 1922
Ronald DeLord, Combined Law Enforcement Associations of Texas, *The Ultimate Sacrifice*
John Lewis, Eddy County, New Mexico, Sheriff's Department
Sammy Tice, *Texas County Sheriffs*
Captain James B. Williams, Carlsbad Police Department

Jamison Ranch, Colfax County
1909

Deputy Killed by Horse Thieves Near Folsom
Jamison Brothers Arrested, Charged
Posse Rides 200 Miles in Record Time

A band of horse thieves busily plied their trade in northwestern Union County, New Mexico in the spring of 1909. In one case alone, they stole 28 head from the ranch of John King near Folsom, but many other ranchers suffered losses of riding stock. In early June, Sheriff D. W. Snyder learned that some of the stolen horses had been sold to farmers around Richland in southwestern Kansas, and he immediately sent his deputy, Jim Kent, to Kansas to see what he could find. Kent located and recovered many of the horses and learned that others had been traded for mules and other horses. He picked up a trail in Richland that took him to Trinidad, Colorado. Kent learned there that a man named Clarence Hamilton had sold the mules and horses to a Colorado farmer.

When Hamilton went to a Trinidad bank with the farmer to close the deal and collect, he found Deputy Kent waiting for him. It didn't take long for Hamilton to tell Kent that the Jamison brothers actually stole the animals. The Jamisons maintained a "camp" in eastern Colfax County, near the Union County line, only about five miles from the King ranch.

Sheriff Snyder dispatched Deputies Kent, H. M. Williams and Gay Melon to arrest the Jamison brothers. The posse reached the King ranch on the evening of July 1 and spent the night there. It was still dark the next morning when the posse took the trail to the Jamison place, and the officers took positions of concealment outside the small adobe before daylight. Shortly, one of the Jamisons exited the house to gather kindling and firewood for use in preparing breakfast. Deputy Kent followed him back inside and at gunpoint ordered, "Throw up your hands!" Kent's demand was immediately answered by a gunshot from an adjoining room. Kent, shot in the neck, fell to the floor, mortally wounded. Deputy Williams then approached the door and he too was shot and severely wounded. Deputy Melon hurried away from the scene and back to the King ranch for help. Williams, in great agony from a stomach wound, was able to reach his horse and mount, and he too started for the King ranch. His strength failed him, however, and he collapsed along the road where a second posse from Folsom found him, unconscious from loss of blood.

News accounts of the time reported that the Jamisons stepped over and around Kent's body as they finished preparing and eating breakfast. Then they mounted up and rode west, toward Ratón, but apparently not in great haste.

Meantime, Melon reached the King ranch and John King rode to Folsom where he sent a telegram to Sheriff Snyder:

> July 2, 9:00 a.m.
> Sheriff: J. I. Kent killed at Jamison ranch. Take along
> posse from there overland at once.

Sheriff Snyder and a three-man posse set out from Clayton immediately, and by riding hard overtook the killers about midnight at the George ranch, only 20 miles from the scene of the killing. One story is that the Jamisons surrendered themselves to Mr. George, who was a Justice of the Peace. Other accounts are less clear as to what the out-

95

laws were doing at the George place.

The officers and their prisoners began the trip back to Clayton at once, and arrived there at noon the next day. The Sheriff and his posse had covered a distance of more than 200 miles in about 29 hours.[1] The Jamisons were locked in jail, and when another brother, and their father, arrived from Ratón to visit them, they were arrested, too.

Deputy Williams survived a long wagon ride in the hot sun to Folsom where a local doctor dressed his wound. The morning train then took him to Trinidad, Colorado, where the bullet could be removed.

Local newspapers reported that James I. Kent was born in Bartols County, Texas in 1875. Maps contemporary to the times, as well as modern references, do not show any such county in Texas.

Kent's obituary said this:

> He was a highly esteemed citizen, doing right by his fellow man for the sake of doing right, a friend to those for whom he professed friendship. His untimely death we greatly deplore and realize that one has been called from our midst whose place in our community will be hard to fill.

Complete details regarding the prosecutions of the Jamison brothers are not known. It is known that George Jamison was convicted of manslaughter for killing Deputy Kent, and sentenced to five years in the Penitentiary.

ENDNOTE:

[1] Simple arithmetic reveals that the posse averaged nearly seven miles per hour, which was pretty speedy traveling in those days. A ride of 50 to 60 miles per day on horseback was generally considered a day's work.

SOURCES:

Albuquerque *Morning Journal,* July 3 & 4, 1909
Clayton *Citizen,* July 2 & 9, 1909
Mrs. N. H. Click, *Us Nesters in The Land of Enchantment*
Lee Johnson, Sheriff, Union County, New Mexico, October 22, 1999

Lake Valley, Sierra County
1870s/1880s

Mining Town Claims a Gunfight a Day
Or Maybe Not
Richest Silver Mine in New Mexico

"Lake Valley is the toughest town I've ever seen. I'm satisfied a man died with his boots on every night."

So said a surveyor named Parker as quoted by old-time Hillsboro resident George Meyers.[1] While there is little doubt that Lake Valley was a violent place to live in the late 1870s and 1880s, Parker's assertion is probably a bit exaggerated.

There are a couple versions of the town's origins, but they both agree that George Lufkin made the first silver discovery in the area in 1878. One source says the place was originally named Daly for George Daly, who had been killed by Apaches. Another says that Lufkin sold his find to George Daly, a member of a Colorado syndicate, and that Daly was killed by marauding Apaches in the early 1880s. In any event, the name Daly did not stick and some folks called the place Sierra City. Because there was a small lake nearby, the name Lake Valley was of-

Lake Valley, New Mexico, ca. 1890.

ficially adopted when the Post Office was established in 1882.

The silver deposits found in the Lake Valley district were the richest in all of New Mexico. One of the earliest mines was the Sierra Grande, which produced more than $700,000 worth of bullion in six months. The largest of them all was named the Bridal Chamber. So large was it that a railroad spur line was built directly into the mine to facilitate removal of the ore and to keep production costs low. One source says there was so much exposed silver that one could hold a candle to the wall and it would actually melt. Another source reported that the walls of the grotto were almost pure silver. Three-million dollars was extracted from the Bridal Chamber.[2]

There was indeed trouble with the Apaches—Victorio, Nana and Loco in particular. George Daly was killed when he accompanied a troop of cavalry that was ambushed by the Apaches. Five others were also killed, including the officer in command of the soldiers. Indians never attacked the town Lake Valley, but several ranches in the area were set upon by the hostiles. One source reports that of the 33 graves at Lake Valley at one time, Indians had killed 28. (Hardly an indication that a man per night was being killed in the community.)

Lake Valley and other towns in the area—Kingston and Hillsboro—also became centers for rustler gangs. Probably the most significant outlaw bunch was led by John Kinney. According to the Santa Fe *New Mexican*, the thieves were "running off oxen of farmers in the Mesilla Valley so they cannot plow and the country is a wasteland." Major Albert Jennings Fountain was charged with putting a stop to the depredations. He implemented a multi-pronged attack and soon began arresting rustlers and by March 1883 he had many of them in custody, including John Kinney. But that was not an end to the problem. Members of the Kinney gang were still seen in and around Lake Valley.

Doña Ana County Prosecutor Albert Jennings Fountain. After Twitchell.

Fountain wasted no time in moving his troops from Las Cruces, first to Nutt Station, and then north to Lake Valley. He ordered another company of his troopers, under Francisco Salazar, to head for Kingston. Both companies were successful in rounding up the remaining rustlers before they rendezvoused back at Nutt Station. This finally broke the back of the criminal organization.

Just over two years later, in May 1885, Fountain, by then promoted to colonel, was back in Lake Valley. He established regimental headquarters there as troops under his command sought out Apaches, many of them under Geronimo, who had been raiding in the area. One source says this about that effort: "Almost at once, the number of reports of killings and property losses began to drop, and after June 30 no casualties due to Indian raids were reported in the entire protective zone patrolled by his First Regiment."[3]

And while all this was going on, legend holds, efforts were made by townspeople to put a lid on the violence by hiring Timothy Isaiah "Longhaired Jim" Courtright as town marshal.[4] One source says this; "hired as town marshal, [Courtright] engaged several lawbreakers in gun battles and things began to settle down." The problem is that no other historian reports that Courtright was ever marshal in Lake Valley. He was an ore guard for the American Mining Company, and he did kill a couple of would-be robbers, but that was the extent of his efforts toward law and order. He later murdered two squatters for a rancher, and former Union General, named John Logan. He left New Mexico with the law on his heels.[5]

Courtright is only interesting to western history buffs because on February 8, 1887 he engaged in a gunfight with gambler Luke Short in Fort Worth, Texas, and came up wanting. The two guns he habitually carried did not prevent Short from putting three bullet holes in him.

Historians generally agree that at its peak, Lake Valley had a population of 3,000 to 4,000 souls, although one claims only 1,000. Whatever it was, as the silver mines played out, the population dwindled until the place became a classic ghost town. What remains of it today is partly on private land and is overseen by the Bureau of Land Management. A caretaker resides in the village and self-guided tours are available.

ENDNOTES:

[1] This quote is taken from *Ghost Towns of New Mexico, Playthings of the Wind* by Michael Jenkinson with photos by Karl Kernberger. Unfortunately, references are not provided and so the date of the comment is not reported, nor is further information about the surveyor. UNM Press published the book in 1967.

[2] A single chunk of silver ore from Lake Valley, valued at $7,000, was dis-

played at Denver in 1882.

[3] *The Life and Death of Colonel Albert Jennings Fountain*, A. M. Gibson, Univ. of Oklahoma.

[4] Courtright's hair was really not very long, especially for his times. It did not reach his collar. Wild Bill Hickok's hair was much longer.

[5] Courtright returned to New Mexico a couple of years later, faced trial on the murder charges, and was acquitted before he returned to Texas to meet his fate at the hands of Luke Short.

OTHER SOURCES:

Francis & Roberta Fugate, *Roadside History of New Mexico*

Robert Julyan, *The Place Names of New Mexico*

Denis McLoughlin, *An Encyclopedia of the Old West*

Leon Metz, *The Shooters*

Bill O'Neal, *Encyclopedia of Western Gunfighters*

Marc Simmons, "Ghosts of Lake Valley Tell a Tale," *Prime Time*, August 2003

"Visions from the Past," Bureau of Land Management, Las Cruces Field Office

Las Cruces, Doña Ana County
1895

Gun Play on Main Street — Shots Fly Hither & Yon
Ben Williams, Joe Morgan Wounded
No One Killed, Williams Arrested

Ben Williams is not a name frequently mentioned in the annals of the Old West, and yet he served at various times as Deputy U. S. Marshal, Doña Ana County Deputy Sheriff to Pat Garrett, Las Cruces town constable and chief special agent for the Santa Fe Railroad.[1] He played major roles in several significant episodes of his time, and he engaged in several life-threatening confrontations.

Williams was born in France in 1861[2]. He is believed to have arrived in the United States in 1873. Not much is known of his early life, but by the late 1880s he was working as a bill collector for the Singer Sewing Machine Company in and around Las Cruces. This occupation was described as "challenging work" at the time.

By 1890 he was self-employed as a detective in El Paso. He was hired to secure the release of Dr. William Bolton from jail in Juarez, Mexico where he was being held on a murder charge. It was not possible for him to do by legal means, or by bribery, so Williams contrived a plan which involved subterfuge to accomplish his goal. Dr. Bolton was able to walk out of the jail unmolested, wearing the uniform of a soldier in the U. S. Army. A group of irate Mexicans offered a large reward for Williams, dead or alive. He never returned to Mexico.

In 1894 he was hired to work as a stock detective for the Southeastern New Mexico Stock Growers Association, for which organization Albert Jennings Fountain served as chief prosecutor. The job afforded him the opportunity to observe Oliver Lee's growing cattle herd. Lee was closely associated with Albert Bacon Fall, Fountain's arch political enemy. Through Fountain's good offices, Williams was appointed Las Cruces town constable, and through the same procedure, Fall had Oliver Lee appointed a deputy sheriff. Lee then went after Williams, with a vengeance.

During the early summer of 1895, Lee arrested Williams for carrying firearms.[3] Williams made bond and was released from custody. On August 16, Lee arrested Williams again, on the same charge. Historian A. M. Gibson[4] tells what happened next:

> Out on bail again, Williams, on the night of September 14, was walking along Main Street [in Las Cruces]. As he fronted Desseur's Building three men stepped from the shadows—Albert Fall and Joe Morgan he recognized immediately; the poor light prevented him from identifying the third party. Morgan put his pistol in Williams face and fired. The constable moved at Morgan's motion; the bullet whined past his temple, but the point-blank blast gave him a bad powder burn. Williams staggered back, threw his left arm over his face, drew with his right, and fired twice at Morgan, one bullet hitting his arm. Fall's shot passed through the crown of Williams' hat. As he returned Fall's shot, Morgan fired again, the bullet entering Williams' left arm at the elbow and passing out the shoulder. The shot spun the constable around. He fired twice at Morgan, hitting

him again, then as he turned and ran for cover across the street, two additional shots were fired at him by the third party still hiding in the shadows.

Fall said later that he and Morgan—Fall's brother-in-law—shot at Williams simply because they didn't like him; that there was no political significance in the matter. It was Williams, however, who was indicted for the shooting affray, though nothing ever came of it. Williams was named chief deputy to Sheriff Numa Reymond the following year.

Through a set of political convolutions, Pat Garrett was named chief deputy the same year—Sheriff Reymond left town for an extended European vacation—and Ben Williams continued as Garrett's right-hand man. Garrett was elected in his own right in 1898 and Williams was once again chief deputy. In this capacity, Williams faced his next formidable challenge.

Garrett's primary goal was to solve the mystery of the disappearance of Col. Fountain and his son, Henry, which had occurred in February 1896. The investigation led to suspects Oliver Lee, Jim Gilliland and Bill McNew. Warrants were issued and McNew was soon arrested. Lee and Gilliland managed to avoid arrest by staying away from Las Cruces and visiting various ranches in Tularosa Basin. In July 1898, two of Garrett's deputies, Clint Llewellyn and José Espalin, discovered that Lee and Gilliland were visiting the Cox Ranch on the east slope of the Organ Mountains. They also learned that the wanted men would soon be riding east, to Lee's Wildey[5] Well Ranch.

Garrett assembled a posse made up of himself, Llewellyn and Espalin, Ben Williams and Kent Kearney. All were described as experienced gun-hands, except for Kearney who was a former schoolteacher. The posse trailed the outlaws to the Wildey Well ranch. The particulars vary widely regarding what happened next. Garrett's version held that the officers learned from people inside the house that Lee and Gilliland were hiding on the roof of the adobe structure.[6] The sheriff ordered Llewellyn to guard the people inside the house while he positioned

Deputy U.S. Marshal Ben Williams

Williams under a water tank. Garrett, Kearney and Espalin would ascend a ladder to the roof. Kearney went first and peered over the parapet to discover the posse's quarry. Garrett claimed that he demanded surrender at that point[7]. The response was gunfire from the roof, and Kearney was severely wounded in the shoulder and groin and fell to the ground. All the remaining deputies returned fire but Lee and Gilliland had the positional advantage. Espalin sought cover along a wall and had no opportunity to continue firing. Williams returned fire, aiming at rifle flashes, but the wanted men shot holes in the tank he used for concealment. He was obliged to remain in place and be soaked with water.

This episode was probably Garrett's most humiliating setback. He was forced to retreat from the ranch empty-handed, and Kent Kearney died in the unsuccessful effort.[8]

Williams continued to serve with Doña Ana County Sheriff's office until 1901 when he took a position as Special Agent with the Atchison, Topeka & Santa Fe Railroad. He remained with the Santa Fe for many years, and rose to the rank of Chief Special Agent. He was involved in a number of incidents that involved gunplay and his son credited him with running the KKK out of El Paso. He was described as a quiet, well-mannered, well-dressed man who did not look the part of gunfighter. He is reported to have been married "about" eight times, and to have fathered two children, a son and daughter. He was also said to have been "…still looking at girls up until 1934."

Upon his retirement, he opened a detective agency in El Paso. He died there in 1935 of cancer. He'd invested all his money in bank stock, and the Great Depression had wiped him out. He died penniless.

ENDNOTES:

[1] One list of "gunslingers" in far west Texas and southern New Mexico in the 1890s lists Williams along with such notables as Bat Masterson, John Wesley Hardin, John Selman and Pat Garrett.

[2] According to one source, his own son believed him to have been born in Ireland, but his death certificate shows place of birth as France.

[3] Some sources indicate that it was perfectly legal for Williams to be armed.

Others say it was technically illegal.
[4] Quoted from *The Life and Death of Colonel Albert Jennings Fountain*, University of Oklahoma Press.
[5] Also spelled *Wildy*.
[6] It was not unusual at the time for people to sleep on flat roofs of adobe houses during the summer time. It was much cooler than sleeping inside.
[7] Oliver Lee claimed later that Garrett and his posse began firing at him and Gilliland without any warning.
[7] Lee and Gilliland were arrested later, tried and acquitted of killing Henry Fountain.

SOURCES:

Larry Ball, *Desert Lawmen, The High Sheriffs of New Mexico and Arizona, 1846-1912*

H. B. Hening, Ed., *George Curry, 1861-1947, An Autobiography*

William A. Keleher, *The Fabulous Frontier*

Leon Metz, *Pat Garrett, The Story of a Western Lawman*

R. A. Suhler, "Ben Williams, Lawman," *Password* (Publication of the El Paso County Historical Society), Vol. XXVII, spring 1982

Martha Plotner Williams, correspondence, July 8, 1982

Dave Mather

Las Vegas, San Miguel County
1880

Mysterious Dave Mather Shoots
His Way to Fame in Gunfight with Thugs
Fades into Dim Recesses of History

Many western history buffs consider Mysterious Dave Mather one of the most enigmatic characters in the history of the Old West. Within the context of the times it was easy for him to foster a shadowy image by reticence and even deceit. He was, after all, as much a con-man as a gun hand. Most western history writers have something to say about Mather, and with some exceptions, they generally agree about his exploits. In his own time, lawmen in Arkansas, Texas, Kansas and New Mexico knew him all too well. The only real mystery about Mather has to do with what became of him.

Dave is said to have been a direct descendent of the 17th and 18th century Puritan preachers Increase (1639-1723) and Cotton (1663-1728) Mather. One source says he was actually descended from Timothy Mather, Cotton's uncle. This source reports that Mysterious Dave—David Allen Mather—was born in Connecticut on August 10, 1851 to

Wyatt Berry Stapp Earp

Ulysses W. Mather and the former Lydia E. Wright.[1] His brother, Josiah "Cy," was born in October 1854. A third brother lived less than a year.

In 1868, "Davey" and Cy ran away to sea, but that didn't last long. They both jumped ship in New Orleans in 1870 and went their separate ways. No one seems to know exactly what happened in the interim, but "New York" Dave — as he was called early on — was involved in cattle rustling with two other men in Arkansas, in 1873: Dave Rudabaugh and Milt Yarberry[2]. Lawmen chased all three of them to Texas for thievery and alleged participation in a murder in Sharps County. For a short time, it appears that Dave Mather hunted buffalo on the plains of West Texas.

He appeared in Dodge City some time in 1874 and was soon involved in an altercation with a gambler that left him with a severe knife wound to the stomach. Few folks around town expected him to survive, but a Dr. McCarthy, using a pool table for an operating table, and whiskey for an anesthetic, sewed Mather up. After Dave became a Dodge City policeman, he'd "persuade" gamblers, prostitutes and others to visit Doc McCarthy for the purpose of a physical examination, the cost of which was five dollars. McCarthy acknowledged some years later that the practice wasn't exactly ethical. He also noted that he needed the money.

In 1878, Mather showed up in Mobettie, Texas with another former Dodge City policeman named Wyatt Earp. The two of them were selling "gold" bricks they claimed had been found in an old Spanish mine. The scam might have worked had they not sold one of the phony

110

bricks to the sheriff. He discovered the fraud and escorted the bunko artists out of the county. Mather may have killed a man in Mobettie, but that is not confirmed.

Dave returned to Dodge City, but it wasn't long before he became mercenary gunman for the Santa Fe Railroad in the so-called Royal Gorge War in Colorado. Among the other hired guns in that dispute was his old friend Dave Rudabaugh, as well as Doc Holliday and Bat Masterson. Nothing much came of the matter and Dave appeared in Las Vegas, New Mexico in 1879 where he soon became a deputy marshal.

His reputation as a gunman really took root in Las Vegas. His first shooting, in November, was of a soldier who attempted to flee custody. Dave shot him in the thumb and shoulder. In January 1880, Mather was present in the Close and Patterson Saloon when four young toughs shot deputy marshal Joe Carson nine times. Mather pulled his guns and opened fire. When the smoke cleared, one of the killers was dead, another badly wounded. The other two were less seriously injured[3]. Mather is believed to have led the lynch mob that took the killers out of the jail a week or so later. All three were summarily executed.

Also in January of that year, Dave killed a railroad worker named Joe Castello in a street gunfight. He resigned his position in March.

Mather returned to Dodge City but didn't stay long. Early the following year he was arrested in San Antonio, Texas, for passing counterfeit money. He was acquitted of that charge and was next in Dallas where he was arrested for stealing jewelry from a prostitute. He spent three months in jail before he was tried and acquitted of those charges, too.

He next appeared in El Paso. One source says he served as a deputy marshal under Dallas Stoudenmire. Another says he served under Marshal Jim Gillett. Both appointments were unlikely and in any event, he did not make a name for himself in West Texas.

By mid-1883 Mather was back in Dodge City where he was appointed both deputy town marshal and Ford County deputy sheriff. He was also a partner in the Opera House Saloon. Nothing was to last with Dave. In the spring of the next year, a new city administration took office and one of the first orders of business was to replace Dave Mather with Tom Nixon, an old buffalo hunter and competing saloonkeeper. To complicate matters further, word around town was that Dave and Nixon's wife had an intimate relationship. One night, in an alley near the Opera House Saloon, Nixon took a shot at Mather, and missed. Dave declined to press charges so Nixon went free. Three days later, Mather came upon Nixon on the street. Nixon tried to pull his own gun, but before he could, Mather shot him, four times. Mather was acquitted of murder charges.

After 1885, Dave drifted out of the public eye. He turned up briefly in New Kiowa, Kansas and then again in Long Pine, Nebraska. A body matching his description was found along a railroad in Texas in 1886, but it was never positively identified. Some believe that he moved along to Canada where he joined the Royal Canadian Mounted Police and lived until 1922. The RCMP denies that he was ever a member.

Most absurd is the story about Mather being part of a posse that pursued an unidentified flying object from Arizona to Mexico in 1889. Mather, the story goes, rode his horse to a spot where the spaceship had landed and never came back. The UFO lifted off and disappeared over the horizon. Dave was never seen again.

The final mystery of Mysterious Dave will probably never be resolved.

ENDNOTES:

[1] Some sources claim Mather was born in 1845, and in Massachusetts.
[2] Rudabaugh was later sentenced to death for murder at Las Vegas, New Mexico, and Yarberry, who became Albuquerque's first marshal, was hanged there for murder in 1883.
[3] Some sources indicate that two of the killers escaped unharmed. Of course, some sources also omit Mather from this fight entirely. There is little doubt, however, that he was there.

SOURCES:

Howard Bryan, *Robbers, Rogues and Ruffians*
Jon Guttman, "Gunfighters & Lawmen," *Wild West*, December 1994

Dennis McLoughlin, *An Encyclopedia of the Old West*
Leon Metz, *The Shooters*
Bill O'Neal, *Encyclopedia of Western Gunfighters*
Marc Simmons, *When Six-Guns Ruled*
Dan L. Thrapp, *Encyclopedia of Frontier Biography*

Lincoln, Lincoln County
1873

Constable Martínez Killed in Affray
Ben Horrell, Dave Warner & Jocko Gylam
Also Die in Gunplay

Sam, Mart, Merritt, Tom, John and Ben were the Horrell brothers of near Lampasas in central Texas.[1] Some of their neighbors called them "fun-loving cowboys" who regularly shot up the town. They were also the leading members of a group "...whose occupation was the branding, killing and skinning of other people's cattle."

On March 14, 1873, in Jerry Scott's Saloon in Lampasas, Tom, Mart and Merritt, along with their brother-in-law Bill Bowen and several other "cowmen", were confronted by Captain Thomas Williams of the Texas State Police who, along with six officers — one of whom was Black, sought to arrest Bowen.

The Texas State Police of the day were considered a part of the Yankee, carpetbagging regime, and were therefore held in great contempt by southern-sympathizing Texans. The situation was exacerbated in this case by the presence of the Black police officer. Some white Texans considered it an insult to be confronted by a Black policeman, even though in this case he was left outside holding the horses.

In the gunfight that followed, four of the State Policemen, including Capt. Williams, were killed. Mart Horrell and three other men were later arrested and housed in the jail at Georgetown, Texas, between Austin and Waco. On the night of May 2, 1873 the remaining Horrell brothers, and about 30 other riders, stormed the jail and freed Mart and his friends. After that, the brothers rounded up their cattle, sold them and headed northwest to New Mexico.

The Horrell bunch arrived in Lincoln County in the fall of 1873. They bought a homestead/ranch and settled on the Rio Ruidoso not far from the present-day village of Hondo. Other relatives and hangers-on also settled in the area. The county seat at Lincoln was the local hub of activity.

On December 1, Ben Horrell, along with Dave Warner and former Lincoln County Sheriff Jack "Jocco" Gylam, rode into the town of Lincoln. Some said they "undertook to run the town." Others said they simply wanted to carouse in the saloons and brothels. Whatever the reason, they were armed and soon enough they were drunk and shooting their guns. Constable Juan Martínez demanded that they surrender their weapons, and they did. It wasn't long, though, before Horrell, Warner and Gylam were again armed and shooting up a brothel. Constable Martínez and four members of the police guard, accompanied by an interpreter, again confronted the miscreants. As the interpreter began to explain the situation to Horrell and his friends, Dave Warner — who had a long-standing grudge against Martínez — suddenly pulled his pistol and shot the constable, killing him instantly. Warner was killed on the spot by return fire and Horrell and Gylam fled, only to be chased down and also killed by the police guard. Clearly, the officers meant to kill the outlaws: Horrell was shot nine times and Gylam 13 times.

The Horrells did not consider it much of a crime to kill a "Mexican" constable, but they did consider the shooting death of brother Ben murder. Retaliation was swift. A few days after the gunfight in Lincoln, two prominent Hispanic citizens were found murdered on the Horrell ranch. Efforts by Sheriff Alexander Hamilton "Ham" Mills and a forty-man posse to arrest the Horrells failed when they discovered that the Texans had "forted up" in their house on the Rio Ruidoso. A few shots were fired but no one was hit.

On December 20, the Horrells returned to Lincoln and shot-up a wedding *baile*, killing four Hispanic men and wounding one woman. Again, efforts to capture the Horrells were unsuccessful, and other clashes between the Texans and Hispanic citizens occurred.

Warrants were issued, the Army was standing by, and the people were up in arms. The Horrells, no longer welcome in southeastern New Mexico, began a retreat in early 1874, heading back to Texas. Along the way they stole all the horses, mules and cattle they could get their hands on. A Horrell outlaw associate, Edward "Little" Hart, murdered Deputy Sheriff Joseph Haskins at Picacho for no reason other than that Haskins was married to an Hispanic woman. About 15 miles west of Roswell, the Texans encountered five Hispanic freighters doing nothing more than hauling corn, and killed all of them.

Estimates are that the gang killed at least 13, and probably more, Hispanic citizens during the course of the so-called Horrell War of 1873-74.

But Texans were no longer hospitable to the clan, either. Citizens of Lampasas took pot shots at them when they returned to town, but none of the Horrells were killed. By 1876, the Horrell brothers were engaged in a feud with cattleman John Pinkney Calhoun "Pink" Higgins. Higgins shot Merritt Horrell to death in Jerry Scott's Saloon at Lampasas on January 22, 1877.

In 1878, Mart and Tom Horrell were arrested for robbing and killing merchant J. F. Vaughn at a place called Rock School House on Hog Creek in Bosque County. A mob of masked citizens, estimated at 100 strong, stormed the jail at Meridian and killed both outlaws in their cell on December 15, 1878.

Sam, the oldest and quietest, was the last of the brothers. Only he managed to avoid a violent death. It is reported that he returned to

New Mexico in 1880 and moved on to Oregon in 1882. He died peacefully in 1936 at Eureka, California and is buried there.

ENDNOTES:

[1] They were all born in Alabama. The family had moved to Texas by 1867. John Horrell was killed in a gunfight in Las Cruces, New Mexico, before the events described here. The family name is also spelled *Harrell* or *Harrold*, depending on the source.

SOURCES:

Lily Klasner, *My Girlhood Among Outlaws*
Leon Claire Metz, *The Encyclopedia of Lawmen, Outlaws, and Gunfighters*
Frederick Nolan, *Bad Blood: The Life and Times of the Horrell Brothers*
P. J. Rasch, "The Horrell War," *New Mexico Historical Review*, July 1956
C. L. Sonnichsen, *I'll Die Before I'll Run: The Story of the Great Feuds of Texas*

Lincoln Town, Lincoln County
1874

Phillipowsky, Drunk on Town Street
Shot and Killed by William Burns
Inquest Rules Justified Homicide

The following item appeared on the front page of the Santa Fe *New Mexican* in November 1874.

Affray in Lincoln County

A friend gives us the following account of a difficulty at Lincoln resulting in the death of one of the parties. He says a shooting affray took place at Lincoln city, Lincoln county [sic], on the 21st inst. [October 21, 1874], between William Burns and Lyon Phillipowsky, deputy sheriff, which resulted in the death of the latter. Mr. Burns was a clerk in the employ of L. G. Murphy & Co. Phillipow-ski [sic] entered the store late in the evening very much intoxicated and grow [sic] quite insulting to Burns, who attempted to evade any difficulty with him; but the latter drew his pistol threatening Burns' life, and went on the outside and challenged Burns, who procured a pistol and went out.

Phillipowski [sic] commenced firing at him; the latter returned the fire and it was kept up until Phillipowsky fell, mortally [wounded] and died early next morning. The Coroner held an inquest over the body who returned a verdict that Burns was justifiable [sic].

Several historians refer to this affray based on the information provided by the *New Mexican*, but no other details have been discovered. In her autobiography, Lily Klasner refers to a Jewish settler in Lincoln County named Philip Bowski who, she says, became Lincoln County clerk. She makes no mention of this shooting. In the tableau of violence in Lincoln, this appears to have been but a minor incident. It is noteworthy that Phillipowsky's name appears on the monument to fallen peace officers at the Law Enforcement Academy in Santa Fe.

SOURCES:

William A. Keleher, *Violence in Lincoln County, 1869-1881*
Lily Klasner, *My Girlhood Among Outlaws*
Santa Fe *New Mexican*, November 6, 1874
John P. Wilson, *Merchants, Guns & Money, The Story of Lincoln County and Its Wars*

Lincoln, Lincoln County
1878

Sheriff Shot from Cowardly Ambush
Deputy also Wounded, Dies
Assassins Escape After Robbing Body

One of the most cowardly acts of murder in frontier New Mexico took place on April 1, 1878 in the town of Lincoln.

At mid-morning on that day, Sheriff William Brady and deputies George Hindman, Billy Mathews, George Peppin and John Long walked down Lincoln-town's only street.[1] Suddenly from behind cover — either an adobe wall or a heavy gate, depending on who is telling the tale — there erupted a fusillade of small-arms fire. Sheriff Brady was killed instantly, penetrated by numerous bullets. Deputy Hindman also went down, mortally wounded. The remaining deputies scattered and took cover. Billy Mathews was able to return fire, and wounded one of the assailants as he picked over Brady's body.[2] The killers all escaped from the scene.

The question is, who were the assassins?

Historians William A. Keleher and Bill O'Neal identify them as William H. Bonney (Billy the Kid), Henry — or Hendry — Brown, John Mid-

Lincoln County Sheriff William Brady

dleton, Fred Wait— or Waite—and Jim French. To those five, historians John P. Wilson and Robert Utley add Frank McNabb. Billy the Kid historian Don Cline says there were at least 12 men behind the wall, but he does not identify them except for William Bonney and Jim French.

A man named Abneth [sic] McCabe, who lived near Lincoln at the time, wrote the following in a letter to Lily Klasner not long after the events described.

> Now for the War news.... Brady and George Hindman were killed in the streets of Lincoln by men hid in the corral behind the new store of McSween and Tunstall, shot in the back as they were passing. John Middleton, [Robert] Weiderman, a Negro, George Washington, and another Negro, Little Henry, 'the kid' [sic] and a man called French were seen to come out the corral after the firing. All must have shot.

Keleher and Utley are most likely correct, as their scholarship rises to the top in a cauldron full of historians on the subject of the Lincoln County War. It is hard to imagine a dozen gunmen behind that wall, but there were certainly that many, and more, partisans involved in other aspects of the war.

As for Ab McCabe's letter, it is unlikely that Weiderman participated although one writer claims he was there, but did not shoot. Until that date he was a deputy U. S. Marshal. George Washington and George

121

Robinson, both former members of the Negro 10th Cavalry, were arrested after the killings, but most likely had nothing to do with it. So, he seems to correctly list Middleton, Brown, Bonney and French.

Bonney, Brown and Middleton were indicted for the crime. It seems odd that Jim French would avoid indictment since witnesses claimed that he helped Bonney molest the bodies after the killings. Of course, there are those who claimed it was Middleton, not French. In the final analysis, only one man was ever convicted for killing Sheriff Brady, and that was Bonney. He claimed that he did not fire a fatal shot since he spent his time shooting at Billy Mathews, a man with whom he had a personal grudge.

What became of the other known shooters?

Frank McNabb lasted only one month after the killings. On April 30, he and two others, while watering their horses, were jumped by about two dozen members of Brady's faction. Frank was shot numerous times and his body left where it fell.

Henry Brown returned to Texas by 1880 and became a deputy sheriff. He then moved on to Caldwell, Kansas, where he became the city marshal in 1882. He seems to have been well regarded, and married in March 1884. The following month, his true character emerged. He and his deputy, Ben Wheeler, and two local cowboys attempted to rob the bank at Medicine Lodge, Kansas. Things did not go well. A bank employee went for a gun and was shot dead for his faithfulness to duty. The bank president managed to close the door to the safe, and he too was killed. The robbers got no money.

But that wasn't all. A posse quickly took up pursuit, and the robbers could not find their extra horses. They were soon captured. Back in Medicine Lodge, it wasn't long before a lynch party was formed and when the dust settled, Brown was dead, shot while trying to escape, and the other three were also dead and hanging from a tree.

John Middleton was severely wounded in the gunfight at Blazer's Mill four days after Brady's assassination. He recovered at Fort Sumner and then migrated to Kansas where he entered the grocery business. In 1885 he'd moved on to Oklahoma where he became a consort of famed

122

lady outlaw Belle Starr. Her husband, Sam, seems to have been away at the time, but maybe not. Someone shot and killed Middleton from ambush in May 1885. It is noteworthy that Belle was shot from ambush and killed less than four years later.

Fred Waite lasted a little longer. Fred was a quarter-blood Cherokee. After the killings, he remained with Bonney for a few months, but ultimately returned to the Cherokee Nation in Oklahoma. He became the tax collector. He died in 1895, at age 42, of unknown causes.

And no one knows what became of Jim French. He too remained with Bonney for a time and probably participated in some cattle rustling. But at some point he and the Kid parted ways and French drifted off into obscurity. In one of those odd historical coincidences, at this exact same time, one Lt. James H. French was stationed at nearby Fort Stanton, and he sided with Brady. Apaches killed him in 1880.

And William H. Bonney? Everyone knows that he was shot and killed by Sheriff Pat Garrett at Fort Sumner, New Mexico, late on the evening of July 14, 1881.

ENDNOTES:

[1] Historian Don Cline claims they were all on horseback.
[2] Some writers claim the assassin only intended to steal the sheriff's rifle; others that he was after a warrant that Brady carried in his coat pocket.

SOURCES:

Eve Ball, Ed., *Lily Klasner, My Girlhood Among Outlaws*
Donald Cline, *Alias Billy the Kid, The Man Behind The Legend*
Elvis E. Fleming, *J. B. "Billy" Mathews, Biography of a Lincoln County Deputy*
William A. Keleher, *Violence in Lincoln County*
Bill O'Neal, *Encyclopedia of Western Gunfighters*. University of Oklahoma Press
Robert M. Utley, *High Noon in Lincoln, Violence on the Western Frontier*
John P. Wilson, *Merchants, Guns & Money: The Story of Lincoln County and Its Wars*

Lincoln, Lincoln County
1878

Young Yginio Salazar Wounded in Gun Battle
Half Dozen Other Men Die
McSween House Burns

The Lincoln County War in New Mexico began, more or less officially, on February 18, 1878 when Englishman John Tunstall was murdered by deputies of Sheriff William Brady. There were several skirmishes between then and July, when the war's major battle took place in the town of Lincoln. By then, matters had reached the boiling point and it seemed clear that a major confrontation was unavoidable.

On the evening of Sunday, July 14, the forces which represented Alexander McSween rode into Lincoln and a contingent of them "forted up" in McSween's house on the town's only street. Among the gunmen was New Mexico's unofficial state outlaw, William H. Bonney, better known as Billy the Kid. The others in the house are less well known: Jim French, Tom O'Folliard, Francisco Zamora, Vicente Romero, Yginio Salazar, and 10 or so others. About 60 McSween men in all were posted around the village.

124

The McSween group was opposed by what was known as the Dolan-Riley faction (or the Murphy-Dolan gang, according to some). At the titular head of their "army" was Lincoln County Sheriff George "Dad" Peppin, who assumed the office after Sheriff William Brady was murdered on April 1. By July 15, Peppin also had 60 or so armed men at his disposal. Sporadic gunfire erupted from time to time, without major damage to either side.

Sheriff Peppin requested help from the U. S. Army at nearby Fort Stanton. Colonel Nathan A. M. Dudley, known for his ability to consume copious amounts of Jimmy Dolan's whiskey, responded

Col. Nathan Augustus Monroe Dudley

on Friday morning, July 19, by sending in 35 men, a Gatling gun, and a mountain howitzer. The balance of power had shifted. Yginio Salazar (his named is spelled variously by historians: Eugenio, Higino, Hijinio), was in the McSween house throughout the siege. He was interviewed by historian Walter Noble Burns many years later. "McSween's orders were not to fire if Peppin's crowd didn't fire. In five minutes after Col. Dudley arrived in Lincoln on July 19, he was talking with Dolan and the others. There would have been no trouble if Dudley had stayed out of Lincoln."

That was probably not the case. By then, Dolan and a number of his cohorts were determined to kill McSween and as many of his associates as possible.

125

By later that day, July 19, without Dudley's help, members of Peppin's posse were able to set fire to the McSween house, and it became clear that the matter would come to a climax as the conflagration raged from room to room. That evening, after McSween himself had been killed, the fighters in his burning house made a mad dash for safety. Billy the Kid, Tom O'Folliard and others made it to safety, but several were shot down by Peppin's posse. Among them was Yginio Salazar. What is interesting about Salazar is that he was only 15 years old at the time.

Years later, Salazar told Burns what happened to him that night, and what he did. "When it came my turn to dart out the door of the McSween house, the Murphy men were firing at a distance of 10 yards. Why we were not all killed, I never could understand. I had not run a dozen steps when I was struck by three rifle bullets—in my hand, the left shoulder, and the left side, the bullet in my side passing entirely through my body. I stumbled, twisted over in the air, and fell on my back among the dead bodies of McSween, Romero, Semora and Harvey Morris. I lay there unconscious for a while. When I came to my senses…it came to me in a flash that my only chance was to play dead, and a pretty slim chance it was…. I lay there motionless for three hours and you must remember that …I was suffering agony…. I crawled away stealthily, making no noise, and got down by the river."

The gunfight took place in the early evening and Salazar managed to reach the home of a relative, about 1,000 yards from the McSween house, by about 9:00 p.m. Dr. Daniel M. Appel was summoned and arrived about midnight and cared for him. The doctor reported later that his wounds, while painful, were not dangerous. Salazar survived his wounds and made a couple of other marks on the history of the Lincoln County War.

When William H. Bonney escaped from custody for the last time, on April 28, 1881, after killing his guards Bob Olinger and J. W. Bell, he stole a horse and rode directly to Salazar's residence, east of Lincoln. Salazar provided the tools and helped the Kid cut off his leg irons.

Salazar lived for more than 50 years after his brush with death. His grave marker reads, "Pal of Billy the Kid." (Note: Salazar's gravesite marker should not be confused with the tombstone in Fort Sumner, New Mexico, which reads "Pals" and marks the place where William H. Bonney (Billy the Kid), Charles Bowdre and Tom O'Folliard are said to be buried.)

SOURCES:

Walter Noble Burns, *The Saga of Billy the Kid*
Maurice G. Fulton, *History of the Lincoln County War*
William A. Keleher, *Violence in Lincoln County*
Michael Wallis, *Billy the Kid: The Endless Ride*
(Note: There are numerous books available on Billy the Kid and the Lincoln County War. Salazar is usually mentioned in passing.)

Oliver Loving

Loving Bend, Eddy County
1867

*Texas Cattleman Oliver Loving Set Upon
By Comanches — Wounded
Dies at Fort Sumner of Gangrene Poison*

One New Mexico historian says this: "In 1867 [Oliver] Loving was wounded by bow and arrow during an Indian attack while on the trail at Loving Bend on the Pecos; he died several days later after reaching Fort Sumner."[1]

There was, however, much more to the story.

Oliver Loving was born in Hopkins County, Kentucky, probably around 1812. He is known to have been living in Lamar County, Texas by 1845 where he did some farming and operated a freight outfit on the side. He seems to have started his cattle-driving career in 1855 when he drove a herd from Colin County to Palo Pinto County, both in Texas. In 1858 Loving and a partner, John Durkee, drove a herd from Texas all the way to Chicago. In 1859 he drove a herd to Denver to take advantage of the market created by the gold mining boom. During the Civil War he sold beef to the Confederacy.

After the war ended, Loving entered into a partnership with the much younger Charles Goodnight (Loving was 54 and Goodnight was 30). Goodnight was a native of Macoupin County, Illinois who had arrived in East Texas as a child. By the time he joined up with Loving, he'd already served as a Texas Ranger and Indian scout. He had amassed his own herd by war's end.

In early 1866, the two men decided to take their combined herds west to the Rio Pecos and then north to Fort Sumner, New Mexico, to sell to the U. S. Army, which had virtually relocated the Navajo Tribe to Bosque Redondo. They arrived in June with a herd of 2,200 head of cattle. This route came to be called the Loving-Goodnight Trail.[2]

Profits were good, so they agreed to bring another herd north in 1867. Loving and Goodnight encountered problems soon after they turned north along the Pecos; Indians harassed them and the herd stampeded, causing delays. Loving decided that he would go to Fort Sumner ahead of the herd to assure the Army that the beef was on the way.

A cowboy named William "One Armed Bill" Wilson[3] accompanied Loving. Before they set out, Goodnight, the experienced Indian Scout, warned them to travel only by night to avoid detection by Comanche Indians roaming the region. For the first couple of days they followed that advice, but seeing no hostiles along their path, they felt safe in traveling in broad daylight. That was a huge mistake. Very soon they were set upon by a Comanche raiding party of about 100 warriors, and they took flight to the banks of the Pecos where they were able to find cover and protect themselves. Both men were well-armed with rifles and pistols and they had plenty of extra ammunition.

When darkness came, one of the Indians, speaking Spanish, shouted an offer to allow the cattlemen to surrender. Both men showed themselves, One-Armed Bill to do the negotiating. But they hadn't any more than done so when the Indians opened fire with rifles. Loving was hit twice, once in the hand and once in the side. Loving convinced Wilson that the cowboy had to get away under cover of darkness and make his way back to the herd and Goodnight.

Wilson, with the disadvantage of having only one arm, and carrying a long-barreled Henry rifle, pulled off a miracle of evasion. By going under water, he was able to slip by three Indians who were actually guarding the river to prevent just such an escape. But then his real ordeal began. He had many miles to go, on foot and barefooted, with no food and no hat across a pitiless barren plain. But he did it! When he finally reached the herd, he was so disfigured by the sun and the elements, that Goodnight would not have recognized him save for his one arm.

A rescue party was organized immediately and set out, but when they reached the spot Loving and Wilson had used for cover, they found Loving gone. There were lots of arrow shafts, but no cattleman. Wilson was convinced that Loving had killed himself rather than face capture by the Comanches, and that his body had been washed down the river. But that wasn't so.

Loving had remained in hiding for two days, but then, in spite of his wounds, he managed to get to the river and he made his escape just as Wilson had. He wandered for three days and was in a daze when a German immigrant and three Hispanic men found him. They took him to Fort Sumner where Goodnight and the rescue party found him several days later.

But Loving's tribulation was not over. He had developed gangrene in his arm, the result of the wound in his hand. One source says that an inexperienced doctor amputated the limb, but made a bad job of it. Another source says the doctor was reluctant to even do the amputation. In any event, gangrene poisoning killed the cattleman three weeks later. Before he died he made Goodnight promise to take his body back to Texas for burial. He said he didn't want to be buried in a "foreign country." Goodnight lived up to his promise and took Loving's body to Weatherford, Texas for final interment.

If all of this sounds a bit familiar, it is because Larry McMurtry used these events for his own purposes in his novel (and later the movie), *Lonesome Dove*. His characters were Woodrow Call (Charles Goodnight) and Augustus McRae (Oliver Loving). Real life and fiction ended in the same way.[4]

The town of Loving, New Mexico, by the way, is named for Oliver Loving. The city of Lovington, New Mexico, is not.

ENDNOTES:

[1] Carole Larson. *Forgotten Frontier: The Story of Southeastern New Mexico.*
[2] Some texts refer to it simply as the Goodnight Trail. It continued north to Denver, Miles City, Montana, and on into Canada.
[3] Wilson lost his arm in a threshing machine accident as a youth.
[4] It is interesting that many Texas history texts do not mention Oliver Loving.

OTHER SOURCES:

Warren A. Beck & Ynez D. Haase, *Historical Atlas of The American West*
Dee Brown, *The American West*
David Pike, *Roadside New Mexico*
Dan L. Thrapp, *Encyclopedia of Frontier Biography*

Martíneztown, Bernalillo County
1886

Wanted Scoundrels Johnson & Ross
Kill Marshal & Deputy in Wild Gunfight
Make Good Their Escape — Avoid Punishment

On Saturday night, November 20th, 1886, Albuquerque Marshal Bob McGuire and his deputy, E. D. Henry, went to Martíneztown, northeast of New Town, to arrest outlaws John "Kid" Johnson and Charlie Ross. The two were members of a gang of robbers and rustlers who had been plying their trade in the area in recent days. The officers held arrest warrants for both, though the specific charges against the two are not known.

Marshal McGuire had received word that the desperadoes could be found hanging around Pasqual Cutinola's dance hall. A search of the establishment was fruitless, but the officers continued looking around Martineztown. They soon found the two outlaws holed up with two young women—Simona Moya and Tercita Trujillo—in a one-room adobe house not far from the dance hall. As the officers made ready to dash through the door, Miss Moya opened the portal and stepped outside for a pitcher of water. McGuire, Henry and the woman fell into a confused heap. The outlaws quickly realized what had happened, grabbed their guns and opened fire. The lamp went out as the officers returned fire and the women took cover under the bed. McGuire was hit in the chest, abdomen and right arm. Deputy Henry was hit twice in the chest and once in the right leg. When a lamp was lit and the smoke cleared, Henry lay dead on the floor. Marshal McGuire was badly wounded, but alive. The outlaws were gone.

Charlie Ross was hit, too. One bullet struck his shoulder and lodged against his shoulder blade and another one grazed his head. He managed to get to his horse, but he only made it a short distance before he collapsed and sought shelter with a woman who lived nearby. A Santa Fe Railroad detective (and former Albuquerque city police officer), Carl Holton, and Police Officer Pete Isherwood tracked Ross to the house which was located in an area of Albuquerque called Hell's half-acre ("...the very worst part of the town—a rendezvous for third-rate harlots and first-class cutthroats and horse thieves," according to the *Albuquerque Morning Journal*). The officers arrested the killer without incident.

Ross claimed later that McGuire and Henry started shooting first, and that he didn't fire his own gun until he had already been shot three times and was flat on the floor with Henry standing over him. Ross also claimed that he had no idea why the officers were after him and Johnson.

Marshal McGuire died of his wounds on November 26, but he remained lucid to the end and was able to tell his version of the gunfight to District Attorney Harvey Fergusson and four witnesses. McGuire, the second Albuquerque City Marshal,[1] was 40 years old at the time of his demise. Newspapers of the time said his death was "...a loss to the town of an honest, effective, and fearless officer and respected citizen." The Marshal's brother took his body back to his native Oswego, New York, for burial.

Henry, a native of Ohio, was buried in Albuquerque.

Charlie Ross recovered from his wounds. On January 3, 1887, he escaped from the Bernalillo County jail. One source says Ross' girl-friend slipped him a key; another says that Ross and jail inmate Peter Trinkaus of Gallup, a convicted murderer, bribed a guard.

Ross left a note addressed to the editor of the Albuquerque *Daily Democrat*:

> County Hotel, January 3, 1887, to Mr. Roberts of the Democrat: Please say in your paper that hearing there is a reward offered for my partner, Johnson, that I have gone to find him. Tell the boys not to feel uneasy about my absence, and as the weather is such that they might take cold, it may be better for their health to stay at home. We'll turn up in time, and don't you forget it.
>
> /S/ C. Henry Ross, with his hair parted in the middle.

Ross was recaptured on January 27 after an attempted train robbery west of Grants and returned to jail in Albuquerque. He escaped again in July 1887, and was never recaptured.

Kid Johnson, described as "...full of cowboy swagger, wears a Chihuahua hat and wears his pants in his boots," received wounds to the neck and foot in the gunfight. He got to his horse and left town, crossing the Rio Grande near Isleta. At the Rio Puerco he joined up with an ox train and the train's captain doctored his foot until he was able to put a boot on and continue his flight. Johnson was later arrested in El Paso on charges of killing the two Albuquerque officers. It was decided that not enough evidence against him existed to justify trial on those charges, and they were dropped. Never tried for the murder of the two officers, Ross and Johnson both lived to old age.

As a result of the Martíneztown gunfight, the Albuquerque *Morning Journal* for November 23, 1886 reported thus:

> The city council are [sic]going to give the policemen latitude hereafter in the use of firearms in making arrests. They have had orders never to use their arms except in case of being fired on. Hereafter any criminal may be

shot by the police if he makes a show of his arms or attempts to use them.

ENDNOTE:

[1] The first Albuquerque Town Marshal was Milt Yarberry, who was hanged for murder on February 9, 1883 in the yard of the Bernalillo County jail.

SOURCES:

Albuquerque *Morning Journal*, Nov. 23 & 27, 1886
Howard Bryan, "Off the Beaten Path," Albuquerque *Tribune*, Nov. 20, 1961
Howard Bryan, *Incredible Elfego Baca*
Marc Simmons, *Albuquerque, A Narrative History*

Mountainair, Torrance County
1933

Son of Sheriff, Billy Meador, Dies
In Mountainair Gunfight
Suspect Jack Layman Escapes — Caught Later

Jack Layman's arrest record began in California where he was arrested for armed robbery three times in the late 1920s. He returned to New Mexico and was soon arrested and convicted of robbing the mayor of Estancia in Torrance County. Freed from prison in the spring of 1933, he took up residence with his mother in Albuquerque.

On the evening of Thursday, July 27, 1933, he and two other men went to Old Albuquerque where they found a bootlegger and got drunk. Deputy Sheriff Frank Mann received a disturbing-the-peace report, and when he tried to arrest Layman and his friends, Layman slashed at the officer with a knife but only managed to cut Mann's shirt. Mann cracked his assailant on the skull with his gun butt, but Layman managed to escape while the deputy arrested the other two men.

Albuquerque officers soon found out who Layman was, and they learned that his mother lived on south Edith Street. They also learned

137

that his brother-in-law, Charles Spencer, owned two residences in Mountainair, Torrance County, at the south end of the Manzano Mountains. When Layman was not found in Albuquerque, Sheriff Felipe Zamora and Deputy Mann, joined by Torrance County Sheriff Rex Meador and his son Billy — who also served as a deputy sheriff — and other deputies, drove to Mountainair.

On Friday evening, after dark, Sheriff Meador, Billy Meador and Torrance County deputy Tom Kane went to the residence occupied by Spencer and his family; while the other officers went to the second residence owned by Spencer. Sheriff Meador described what happened next.

> As we approached the house, Charlie Spencer came out and asked what we were after. I told him we wanted to search his house for a man we had reason to believe was there. Spencer refused on the ground we needed a search warrant, and after 20 minutes argument, Tom Kane was sent back to get such a warrant.

After Kane left, Spencer invited the Meadors inside. As they approached the house, they met Johnny Layman, Jack's 21-year-old younger brother. After a short delay, the front door was opened and they began to enter the house, Johnny Layman going in first, followed by Spencer, then the sheriff, and finally Billy Meador. Just as the sheriff got inside, the lights went out. Rex Meador flicked on his flashlight and spotted Jack Layman coming toward him with a gun in his hand.

"Dad! We've been trapped!" Billy Meador shouted.

Johnny Layman and Charlie Spencer got between Jack Layman and the sheriff and Jack headed for the back door. Billy Meador saw what was happening and ran from the front door and around the house in time to meet Jack Layman as he exited the back door.

"Layman fired first, and immediately afterwards my boy returned the fire. As he fell to the ground he emptied his gun at the fleeing fugitive," Sheriff Meador said.

Charlie Spencer placed himself between the sheriff and the back door, which prevented Rex Meador from firing at Jack Layman as he fled. One of the deputies who had gone to Spencer's other house, however, observed the gunfight between Billy Meador and Jack Layman, and he fired at the fleeing fugitive. One of the deputy's bullets hit Layman in the leg but he none the less made good his escape.[1]

Officers rushed Billy Meador to an Albuquerque hospital while Sheriffs Rex Meador and Felipe Zamora, and Deputy Frank Mann, coordinated a search for Jack Layman. In short order more than 100 officers began combing the scrub pine country south of Mountainair, and by Saturday afternoon more than 200 officers were involved, along with bloodhounds from the state prison.[2]

Billy Meador died at 9:16 p.m. on Saturday. Sheriff Meador stepped from his son's hospital room and called his deputy, Wallace Crawford, in Mountainair. "The boy is dead," he said. "Get that __!"

But that wasn't to be. The search intensified on Sunday and Monday, but Jack Layman couldn't be found. Officers believed at one point that the fugitive had stolen a hobbled horse and made good his escape on horseback. Others suspected that he had help and fled the area in an automobile. Layman's mother thought her son would be found dead in the brush. Sheriff Meador called off the manhunt in the Mountainair area on Tuesday evening, August 1st. Surveillance was maintained at Layman's mother's house in Albuquerque.

On Friday evening, August 4th, exactly one week after he shot Billy Meador, Jack Layman's flight ended. Bernalillo County Sheriff Felipe Zamora, Deputy Frank Mann and two other deputies stopped a car operated by A. N. "Dad" Gragg, an Old Albuquerque bootlegger, on Fourth Street, north of Albuquerque. As officers lifted the cover on the luggage compartment, Layman fired a shot from a .32-20 revolver, which struck no one. Sheriff Zamora immediately tossed a tear gas bomb into the compartment. He also fired a single shot which struck Layman in the finger. Layman surrendered without further ado.

Jack and Johnny Layman, and Charles Spencer were all charged with first-degree murder in the death of Billy Meador. They were tried at Las Cruces on a change of venue in November 1933. Jack Layman was convicted of second-degree murder and sentenced to 75 to 80 years in prison. Johnny Layman and Charles Spencer were acquitted and released.

ENDNOTES:

[1] Jack Layman's mother later claimed that young Meador was shot inside the house, by accident, by one of the officers at the scene, and not by her son, who, she said, was not armed. That theory was largely disproved by the fact that Billy Meador was shot outside the house and Sheriff Meador never fired a shot. The second deputy who did fire at Jack Layman aimed his shots away from the house.

[2] A request for bloodhounds was initially refused because state officials claimed they had no money to pay to transport the dogs, and their handlers, to the Mountainair area. Friends of the Meador family pledged the necessary funds and the dogs arrived on Saturday evening, too late to do any good.

SOURCES:

Albuquerque Journal, July 28, 30, 31; August 2, 3, 5, 6, 7, 8; November 24, 25, 26, 27, 28, 29, 1933

Amarillo Globe, July 31, 1933

Don Bullis, *New Mexico's Finest: Peace Officers Killed in the Line of Duty, 1847-1999*

Organ Mountains, Doña Ana County
1877

Mes Brothers Slain
East of Las Cruces
Local Bad Man Jesse Evans Suspected

To a country where the population density was low, and honest law officers few and far between, came men who'd rather steal than work; who'd rather kill than argue. Such a man was Jesse Evans. (Some sources spell the name *Jessie*.)

He and William H. Bonney — Billy the Kid — were contemporaries, and like the Kid, not much is known about his early life. Not even his name is known for sure. He may also have been Jessie Graham or Will Davis. He was probably born in Missouri about 1853 (which made him six years older than the Kid). He was described as about five-feet seven-inches tall and weighing about 150 pounds. He had gray eyes, light hair and a fair complexion.

He appeared in New Mexico in 1872. He went to work for famed eastern New Mexico rancher John Chisum, and not as a cowboy. He and Jimmy McDaniels, among others, were assigned the task of stealing horses from the Mescalero Apache Reservation. By 1875 he and McDaniels were working for John Kinney on a ranch near Mesilla, in Doña Ana County. Kinney, a native of Massachusetts, had a reputation as a cattle and horse thief, and killer.

On New Year's Eve, 1875, Evans, Kinney and McDaniels went to a dance at Fort Selden. As the evening—and presumably the drinking—progressed, the three of them engaged in a fistfight with some soldiers. They lost and left the party. They returned a few hours later and shot up the place, through a window, killing three people, two of them soldiers. No one was prosecuted for the killings.

On January 19, 1876, Evans shot a former friend named Quirino Fletcher on the main street in Las Cruces; shot him six times and left him laying in the street. He was tried in June of 1877 and acquitted. Later the same year (one source says 1875), Evans and McDaniels shot and killed the Mes brothers, Cruz, Pancho and Roman. The Mes brothers were alleged cattle rustlers, but then so were Evans and McDaniels. Legend holds that the Mes brothers were unarmed at the time they were shot. Nothing came of those killings, either.

Late in 1877, Evans and others were arrested for cattle stealing in Lincoln County, but they escaped custody on November 16. This was at the time when events leading up to the famed Lincoln County war were getting hot. Evans was firmly on the side of Murphy-Dolan and The House, even though he'd previously worked for Chisum, who was solidly in the Tunstall-McSween faction, as was Billy the Kid.

John Tunstall was murdered on February 18, 1878. His killers were Tom Hill, Billy Morton, Frank Baker and Jesse Evans. This event, of course, led to an open shooting war in Lincoln County. On March 9, Billy the Kid killed Morton and Baker. On March 13, Tom Hill was killed while robbing a sheep camp. Evans was wounded at the same time. Even though Billy the Kid vowed to kill everyone involved in the murder of Tunstall, he never made an attempt on Evans. In fact, it was rumored at the time that Jesse Evans was the only man that Bonney feared.

Evans participated in the Five Days' Battle in the town of Lincoln

142

John Tunstall

143

from July 14-19, 1878, and helped in the looting of John Tunstall's store. In an essentially lawless Lincoln County, Evans was an active horse thief and cattle rustler. Along with Bill Campbell and Billy Mathews, he participated in the killing of lawyer Houston Chapman in February of 1879 in Lincoln. Oddly, Billy the Kid was present at the time, too, and he ratted out the other three who were arrested and charged with the crime. Evans and Campbell managed to escape from the Fort Stanton stockade before they could be tried.

Things in New Mexico had become uncomfortably warm for Evans, and he left for Texas where he promptly joined another gang of cutthroats.

In July of 1880, Evans and his gang robbed a store in Fort Davis and fled toward Mexico. A Texas Ranger company chased them to a spot near Presidio where they engaged in a gunfight. Ranger George "Red" Bingham was shot and killed, as was one of the outlaws. The entire gang was captured. Evans was sentenced to two 10-year terms. He arrived at Huntsville Prison on December 1, 1880. He escaped from a work detail on May 23, 1882, and officially disappeared from history. He was never recaptured.

There are several theories about what might have become of Evans. One is that he reverted to his real name, whatever that might have been, and lived out his years as an honest and upright citizen. Another is that he took up with yet another outlaw gang and was killed sometime later.

A third postulation has to do with a book published in 1955 called *Alias Billy the Kid*. In 1950, a man named Ollie L. "Brushy Bill" Roberts emerged from obscurity and claimed to be Billy the Kid. The book does not prove Roberts' point; but it does prove that Roberts, under whatever name, was present in Lincoln County during the hostilities in the late 1870s. He knew too much about the war not to have been a part of it.

So who, then, was he? Roberts may have been Jesse Evans, and for several reasons. First of all, the only Anglo involved in the war who could not be accounted for after the shooting stopped was Evans. And

144

then there was the matter of their descriptions, which were very similar, down to and including the shape of their ears. And finally, in spite of all that Roberts had to say about the players in the Lincoln County War drama, he had nothing even remotely bad to say about Evans. At one point Roberts, as the Kid, even says this: "You know Jesse and I were nearly like brothers." An unlikely comment. But even more telling is the fact that Roberts ignored the fact that Evans participated in the killing of John Tunstall. The Kid would certainly have had something to say about the murderer of his "best friend."

And why would Evans, as Roberts, call himself Billy the Kid instead of using his own name? Probably because in 1950 not many people had ever heard of Jesse Evans, while Billy the Kid had become something of a folk hero. If he craved public attention, he surely got more as Billy than he would have as Jesse Evans.

What is really known is that Brushy Bill Roberts died on December 27, 1950 in Hico, Texas. Whatever he knew about Jesse Evans, if anything, went to the grave with him.

SOURCES:

Elvis E. Fleming, *J.B. "Billy" Mathews, Biography of A Lincoln County Deputy*
William A. Keleher, *Violence in Lincoln County*
McCright & Powell, *Jessie Evans: Lincoln County Badman*
Sonnichsen & Morrison, *Alias Billy the Kid*
Dan L. Thrapp, *Encyclopedia of Frontier Biography*
Robert Utley, *Four Fighters of Lincoln County*

Puerto de Luna, Guadalupe County
1880

Sandia Mountain Desperado Looses
Gun Affray with Sheriff Pat Garrett
Survives Wound — Fined $80

Patrick Floyd Garrett (1850-1908) is New Mexico's most famous lawman, even though he only served in that capacity for six or so of his 58 years. Over the years, though he was involved in a half-dozen or more incidents that involved gunplay, but only one of them could by any means be considered a duel. There was certainly no duel involved on the night of July 14, 1881 when he killed William H. Bonney in a darkened bedroom at Fort Sumner, New Mexico. By November 1880, Garrett had been elected sheriff of Lincoln County, New Mexico. While he would not take office until January 1, 1881, he immediately took to the trail of Billy the Kid. That had been the promise upon which his campaign for sheriff was based.

In early December, Garrett and a posse ran into Tom O'Folliard, one of Billy's gang, and a brief skirmish ensued. No one was injured. A short time later, in the same area, not far from Fort Sumner, Garrett

Lincoln County Sheriff Patrick Floyd Garrett

and his friend Barney Mason took a couple of prisoners—J. J. Webb, a murderer, and George Davis, a horse thief—into custody. Both had escaped jail at Las Vegas. Garrett and Mason took them to the village of Puerto de Luna where they turned their charges over to deputies from San Miguel County. They went to Alejandro Grezelachowski's store and saloon for a drink.

A local bad man, Marino Leyba, who came to be called the Sandia Mountain Desperado, entered the establishment and loudly declared, "By God, even that damned Pat Garrett can't take me!"

"I don't want anything with you. I have no warrant to arrest you," Garrett replied.

Leyba continued to verbally abuse Garrett as he went outside, and Garrett followed him to the portal where he gave the outlaw a shove which sent him sprawling into the dust on the street.

"Get away from here!" Garrett ordered.

According to Historian Leon Metz, "Humiliated, the Mexican gunman reached for his pistol, and although he beat Garrett to the draw, his shot went wild. At almost the same instant Garrett's .45 roared, but he too was hasty, and the slug merely kicked up dust at the rowdy's feet. Pat then fired a second time with more finesse. The bullet shattered Leyba's left shoulder blade."

There are, of course other versions having to do with the number of shots fired, and the exact wording of the insults.

Leyba fled the scene and one legend holds that Garrett stopped Barney Mason from killing Leyba with a rifle. Another version holds that Mason fired at Leyba as he fled down the road, but missed.

Leyba was arrested in 1881 and tried in August of that year for shooting with intent to kill one Patrick F. Garrett. A jury convicted him in the matter, and fined him $80.

The Sandia Mountain Desperado was shot down and killed on March 29, 1887 by Santa Fe County sheriff's deputies Joaquin Montoya and Carlos Jacome a few miles from Golden, New Mexico. He was not quite 30 years old.

148

SOURCES:

Howard Bryan, *Robbers, Rogues and Ruffians*
Leon C. Metz, *Pat Garrett, The Story of a Western Lawman*
Bill O'Neal, *Encyclopedia of Western Gunfighters*
Marc Simmons, *Ranchers, Ramblers and Renegades*

Ratón, Colfax County
1882

Drunkard Goes on Shooting Spree
Four Killed Including Judge Moulton
Gus Mentzer Hanged From Signpost After First Effort Fails

Gus Mentzer, 24, worked as barkeeper for William "Billy" Burbridge, a gambler who owned and operated the Bank Exchange Saloon[1] in Ratón, New Mexico. Burbridge fired Mentzer for drinking and carousing and Mentzer left town for a time. On the evening of Monday, June 26, 1882, he came back. Mentzer, drunk and armed with pistols provided by another gambler, named Turner, approached Deputy Sheriff Pete Dollman on the street in front of the Bank Exchange Saloon. He pulled one of the guns and jammed it against the deputy's ribs.

"Give up your gun," Mentzer demanded.

"Oh, no, I could not do that," Dollman replied.

"But you must!"

About then a citizen named Johnson got close enough to knock Mentzer's hand downward and the gun discharged harmlessly into the dusty street. Mentzer ran to the front door of the Bank Exchange

The Raton Guard, June 30, 1882 story on the hanging of Gus Mentzer

Saloon. Deputy Dollman fired several shots in his direction, all of which missed except the one that struck a citizen named W. H. Harris, who just happened to be hurrying along the sidewalk. Mentzer escaped into the saloon, then fled out the back door.

Dollman and a group of citizens searched the town, but Mentzer was not to be found. At about 9:00 p.m. the young gunman appeared at the Bank Exchange Saloon and ordered a drink. Whether he got it or not is unrecorded. Deputy Dollman was present in the saloon and he and other citizens chased Mentzer into the street and began shooting at him. The fugitive fled toward the railroad depot where he shot and wounded J. H. Latimer in the leg and breast. He jumped aboard a railroad engine that had its steam up, but he couldn't make the giant vehicle move. Citizens S. H. Jackson and Hugh Eddleston approached the engine.

"There he is," Jackson shouted an instant before Mentzer shot and killed him. Eddleston was killed a few seconds later.

Deputy Dollman and another deputy, William Burgen, were then able to capture Mentzer, whose gun was empty. They took the prisoner to the Little Brindle Saloon where he was left in the charge of Deputy Burgen behind a locked door. Burgen went about putting leg irons on the prisoner while Dollman went to the telegraph office to wire the bad news to S. H. Jackson's widow.

One of Mentzer's victims, Hugh Eddleston, had been a business partner of Justice of the Peace Harvey Moulton, and the judge soon arrived at the saloon where Mentzer was being held. He banged on the door, but Burgen would not let him in. Moulton kicked the door opened and entered, gun in hand.

"Give up the son of a ----- to be hung!" he ordered, according to a witness.

Burgen refused, citing his duty to protect the miscreant.

As Moulton made a grab for the prisoner, Burgen fired and the judge only lived long enough to fire a single shot into Burgen's stomach. Mentzer escaped and fled to the Williams and Frick butcher shop where Deputy Dollman arrested him yet again. The young killer begged Dollman to protect his life and the deputy said he'd do his best, but Dollman must have known his efforts would be futile. The butcher, Williams, provided a rope and the crowd took Mentzer away from Dollman and told the killer to "say his prayers."

Someone threw the rope over a sign in front of the Raton Bank and the noose was put in place around Mentzer's neck. He "fought like a tiger" as citizens hoisted him up. Then a brace broke and the sign and Mentzer both came tumbling down to the board sidewalk. The crowd was not to be dissuaded. A young boy was boosted up and he placed the rope over the top of a signpost at the corner of Clark Avenue and First Street, and Mentzer was again strung-up. That time it worked. His body was left hanging until Tuesday morning. Later the same day a coroner's jury ruled that "Gus Mentzer came to his death by being hung by the neck by unknown parties."

Deputy Burgen was taken to the offices of the Ratón Coal and Coking Company, where he suffered great agony until he died at 10 o'clock on Tuesday morning. Not a great deal is known about Burgen. A local newspaper described him as an Irishman — a fine looking man, accord-

The hanging of Gus Mentzer

ing to the editor — who lived in Canada for 10 or twelve years before he arrived in Ratón in the spring of 1882. Colfax County Sheriff Allen C. Wallace appointed him deputy sheriff for the coal mining community of Blossburg, five miles northwest of Ratón, less than a week before Moulton killed him. Burgen was only present in Ratón on the day of the Mentzer affair because he'd come to town to visit with his brother who lived there. He was buried at Blossburg on June 28, 1882. "His funeral was largely attended."

The coroner's jury reported thus:

> We ... find that William A. Burgen came to his death by a pistol shot wound received while in the exention [sic] of his duty, fired from a pistol in the hands of Harvey Moulton, Justice of the Peace.

Ratón's citizens were so irate at four killings, two wounded, and one lynching in one night that a mass meeting was held the very next evening. "Ten or twelve hundred" attended, according to the local newspaper. A committee of eleven was named to prevent further disturbance. They issued a report that read in part:

> ...all professional gamblers, footpads, thieves, cappers, dance hall men, bunko men, and all these [sic] who have no visible means of support, as well as all dance house girls and prostitutes generally, are hereby notified and publicly warned to leave this town within 48 hours from 12 o'clock at noon on the first day of July, 1882, and never return under penalty of incurring the just wrath of an indignant and outraged people.

It was never made clear why the gambler, Turner, provided Gus Mentzer with the guns he used to do his evil work. Turner was arrested in Las Vegas during the first week in July, 1882, and removed to Springer where he was tried on unspecified charges. The court fined him $20 and costs and set him free. A Ratón newspaper commented: "Turner will not be likely to show his elegant frame in Ratón again very soon."

ENDNOTE:

1 Some sources indicate that Burbridge and Mentzer were partners in the Bank Exchange Saloon.

SOURCES:

Larry Ball, *Desert Lawmen, High Sheriffs of New Mexico and Arizona, 1846 -1912*

Howard Bryan, "The Gus Mentzer Affair," *Robbers, Rogues, and Ruffians: True Tales of the Wild West*

Don Bullis, *New Mexico's Finest: Peace Officers Killed in the Line of Duty, 1847-1999*

Peter Hertzog, *Outlaws of New Mexico*

Jacqueline Meketa, "Ratón's Black Comedy," *From Martyrs to Murderers, The Old Southwest's Saints, Sinners & Scalawags*

Ratón *Guard*, June 30 & July 7, 1882

Rincon, Doña Ana County
1916

Jail Escapees Shoot, Kill Luna County Sheriff
Outlaw Joe Cranston Also Killed
Others Make Good Escape

Things were astir in Deming on Sunday morning, February 20, 1916. Members of the New Mexico Cattle and Horse Growers Association were beginning to arrive for their annual convention; and the Great Council of the Improved Order of Red Men would also meet in town during the following week.

Things were astir over at the Luna County jail, too.

One cell in the lock-up housed three prisoners: Jesse O. Starr and C. Schmidt, burglars who'd robbed the Palace Saloon, and W. F. Dashley, a forger and embezzler. Jailer Emzie Tabor opened the cell door so Schmidt could empty the chamber pot. The burglar waited until Tabor turned his back to re-open the cell door; then he grabbed the jailer and pinned his arms to his sides. Starr and Dashley helped out. They took Tabor's guns and keys and robbed him of his watch and five dollars in cash. The three outlaws were in control of the jail.

155

They locked Tabor in what had been their cell and unlocked all the other cells. Two prisoners elected to join the little gang in escaping: Francisco Acosta, accused of a murder at Spalding, New Mexico, and Joe Cranston, a vagrant.[1] They then broke into the jail's armory and took rifles, handguns and a large supply of ammunition before they crossed the jail yard and broke into the office where there was a telephone.

Dashley called Del Snodgrass, owner of the Park Garage and Ford Dealership. Posing as an officer, he asked that a car be brought around to the jail so that a sick prisoner could be taken to Faywood Hot Springs, northwest of Deming. Dashley requested a full gas tank and extra tires. He also asked Snodgrass to bring change of a twenty-dollar bill so he could settle up for use of the car right away.

Busy getting ready to provide garage space and automotive services to arriving cattlemen and conventioneers, Snodgrass didn't suspect a thing. He arrived at the jail only to be confronted by five men pointing guns in his direction. He, too, was robbed and locked up with Emzie Tabor. The bandits cut the phone lines, threw the jailhouse keys into a gopher hole, and set off to the northeast toward the town of Rincon, 50 miles away.

Tabor and Snodgrass set up a racket to attract attention to their plight, but no one could hear them. Half an hour passed. Then the wife of one of the prisoners who'd elected to remain in jail arrived for her weekly visit. She freed Tabor and Snodgrass, who soon sounded the alarm.

Luna County Sheriff Dwight Stephens first assumed the outlaws would head for the Mexican border, thirty miles south. He alerted all crossing points by telephone. Then he set about assembling a posse. Witnesses reported seeing the Ford with five men heading northeast, and the six-man posse gave chase in their own machine.[2] The escapees had more than an hour head start, but it wasn't enough. The Deming *Headlight* for February 25, 1916, reported what happened next:

> ...[T]he posse took the trail, finally running on their quarry in a narrow cañon where they had stopped to

156

eat lunch. Deputy Sheriff[s] John T. Kelley and Wayne Estes, who had dropped off the car and had tried to out-flank the outlaws, scrambled to the top of the hill over-looking the cañon where they were seated. At the same time Sheriff Stephens, Buck Sevier and [Deming town] Marshal Tabor came up the cañon, walking to within a few feet of the men before they saw them. Sevier im-mediately ordered them to throw up their hands, but the only reply was a fusillade of shots. Sheriff Stephens dropped at the first exchange of shots, dying instantly, and Sevier received a scalp wound that stunned him, and that came within an ace of taking off the side of his head. From the top of the bluff overlooking the cañon deputy sheriff Kelley, Marshal Tabor, Jack Arnold and Wayne Estes poured a hot fire into the outlaws, wound-ing Starr and killing Cranston. The other three men, Dashley, Schmidt and Acosta broke for the brush and made their escape.

What followed was a manhunt of gigantic proportions. Several carloads of men arrived from Deming along with a U. S. Army detach-ment under Lt. Clyde Earl Ely. Since the gunfight took place in Doña Ana County, Sheriff Felipe Lucero and his posse became active in the search, too.

W. C. Simpson, a cattle inspector, and Fred Sherman, both of Dem-ing, joined Marshal Tabor in the search for Schmidt. They found him at 7:00 o'clock the following morning. He'd made it just sixteen miles, to the east and south of Rincon. He offered no resistance when they arrested him.

Three days later, late in the afternoon, Sheriff Lucero and Las Cru-ces City Marshal Adolfo Sainz picked up Acosta's trail on the Flat Lake Ranch, northeast of Rincon. They followed the fugitive throughout the night, across the San Andres Mountains and into Otero County, a dis-tance of 35 or 40 miles. At noon the following day they located Acosta on the J. B. Baird Ranch. Suffering from hunger and exhaustion, the killer submitted meekly to arrest. He joined Schmidt in the Doña Ana County jail.

Newspapers speculated that the fifth outlaw would be soon captured. One even declared that W. F. Dashley would be back in jail within 48 hours. It wasn't to be.

W. C. Simpson succeeded Dwight Stephens as Luna County Sheriff. He and Doña Ana County Sheriff Lucero kept up the search for Dashley in the weeks and months that followed. At one point, Simpson traced Dashley to Venice, California, but lawmen there failed to act in a timely way and the fugitive escaped. The same thing happened in San Francisco. On August 26, Dashley's luck ran out. Authorities in Reno, Nevada, arrested him and held him for Sheriffs Simpson and Lucero who happily escorted him back to New Mexico.

After Dashley's arrest and conviction, the *Deming Headlight* commented:

> The perfect understanding which exists between the peace officers of Luna, Doña Ana and Grant counties is a powerful aid in the ferreting out of criminals who may be tempted to operate in the southwestern portion of the state, and is an assurance that there is no twilight zone in these parts where outlaws can operate with impunity and feel secure from capture.

In March, 1916, J. O. Starr, C. Schmidt and Francisco Acosta were tried for the murder of Sheriff Stephens. Starr admitted firing shots and seeing Stephens and Sevier fall. He claimed he fired in self-defense after the officers fired first. The jury didn't buy it. Starr was convicted and sentenced to hang. Schmidt was convicted of second-degree murder and sentenced to life in prison. Acosta was acquitted of killing Stephens, but was immediately arrested by Luna County authorities for the killing at Spalding the year before. He was tried and sentenced to 20 years in prison on that charge.

Dashley, whose real name was A. B. Smith, generally considered

158

the leader of the gang and the brains behind the escape, was also convicted of murder in March, 1917 and sentenced to death.[3]

A word is in order about Sheriff Dwight Stephens. A 43-year-old native of Ohio, he'd lived in Deming for about 25 years at the time of his death. First appointed sheriff by Governor Miguel A. Otero in 1904, he served continuously, except for two years, until his death. Sheriff Stephens participated in a gunfight with jail escapees in November of 1911 in which his deputies Tom Hall and A. L. Smithers were killed (see page 30).

Well liked and respected, the Albuquerque *Journal* reported that Stephens' funeral was the largest in Deming history, attended by the entire community.

Fred Fornoff, captain of the New Mexico Mounted Police said this: "Sheriff Stephens was not a gunman in any sense to which odium might attach. The Luna County Sheriff was a fearless man and had a high sense of duty."

ENDNOTES:

[1] The story goes that Joe Cranston was reluctant to participate in the escape but the others persuaded him to go along by promising that he could drive the getaway car.

[2] Automobiles were called *machines* in 1916.

[3] Records do not indicate that either Starr or Smith were ever executed.

SOURCES:

Albuquerque *Morning Journal*, February 21, 22, 24, 25 & 26, 1916

Don Bullis, *New Mexico's Finest: Peace Officers Killed in The Line of Duty, 1847-1999*

Deming *Graphic*, March 16, 1904, February 25 & September 1, 1916

Deming *Headlight*, February 25, & September 8, 1916; March 9 & 23; April 6 & 13, 1917

William Kuehl, Deming Police Department (Ret.)

Rio Puerco, Valencia County
1896

A & P Train Robbery Foiled West of Los Lunas
Brakeman Wounded — Outlaw Killed by Marshal
Thieves Get Loose Change for Their Trouble

The train robbery began at about 7:20 p.m. on October 2, 1896. Seven robbers commandeered A. & P. train Number 2 near the Rio Puerco about 35 miles southwest of Albuquerque.

It was not a smooth operation from the beginning, and one of the outlaws felt called upon to take a few shots at the brakeman and the conductor to gain control of the train. He killed neither, but shot a finger off the brakeman's hand and shattered the man's lantern. The shots got the attention of H. W. "Will" Loomis, a deputy U. S. Marshal who was aboard one of the passenger cars. Loomis had been pursuing one of the robbers and had information that the train would likely be robbed.

Armed with a big bore double-barreled shotgun, the deputy marshal stepped down from the train. He noted a group of men standing near the train's engine, with one man standing apart from the rest. He selected that man as his target and fired. The man staggered and fell to his knees, but regained his feet and disappeared into the darkness. The deputy's second shot hit nothing. The robbers returned the fire — one report says about 30 shots were fired — but they didn't hit anything either. Loomis ducked for cover as a bullet zinged past his ear.

The outlaws, among them Black Jack Christian, acted as if they would go ahead with the robbery in spite of the interruption. They attempted to uncouple the express car from the rest of the train, but they couldn't get it done. Then they discussed using dynamite they'd hidden nearby to blow open the express car door. They were foiled in that plan when several armed trainmen protected the car. Eventually, they abducted the train's fireman and took him some distance from the scene, where they robbed him of his personal possessions, including his tobacco, then let him go.

As they rode away, one of the outlaws called out for his fallen comrade.

"I can't come. I am done for," was the reply from the dark.

The robbers rode on. So much for honor among thieves. All they got for their trouble was what they were able to steal from the fireman and the attention of every lawman in two territories.

The train pulled out for Isleta Junction while Loomis remained behind to search for the body of the man he'd shot. He soon found it, bloody and face down. The outlaw held a six-gun in his left hand. It contained three spent cartridges.

The dead outlaw was one Cole (or Code) Young, also known as Cole Estes and several other aliases. Sources describe him as smallish in stature, five-feet six-inches, or so, and weighing 145 pounds. He was 25 years old at the time of his death. He had $1.45 in his pocket and a receipt showing that he'd bought his hat in Wilcox, Arizona. An autopsy revealed that five buckshot pellets had hit him: four in the chest and one in the face. He'd bled to death.

Thus ended the career of an outlaw who may have been named Cole Young. No one but the undertaker attended his funeral at Fairview Cemetery in Albuquerque, and his grave marker disappeared years ago.

From a modern perspective, Young is only interesting because no

161

one seems quite sure who he really was. One highly-respected source identifies him as Code Young, with Cole Estes as an alias. Another flatly says that his name was Cole Young. After his death, a man from Deming, New Mexico, identified him as Cole Estes and suggested that he changed his name to Young after he left Deming a few months before he was killed, subsequent to a robbery indictment. On the other hand, two railroad workers, who had known him in Trinidad, Colorado, several *years* before his death, officially identified him as Cole Young. Another source says that he may have been wanted by the law in Texas, and his name was not Young *or* Estes, but may have been Bob or Tom Harris.[1]

Gang leader Will "Black Jack" Christian was killed in a gunfight with lawmen about six months later, in April 1897, near Clifton, Arizona, and there was some question about his identity, too. Only one of the remaining Rio Puerco train bandits was officially identified: George Musgrave, alias Jesse Miller, Jesse Williams and Jeff Davis. It seems safe to assume that Will Christian's brother Bob was present, too, but then Bob may not have actually been Will's brother, but rather an Oklahoma killer named Tom Anderson.

What all of this suggests is that some of what is written about the Old West is based on conflicting reports and speculation. One source says that Cole Young rode with Black Jack Ketchum, and that is certainly wrong. Another says that he was killed while hiding on the tender of a train after a failed bank robbery at Nogales, Arizona, nearly a week after he was actually killed in New Mexico. The bottom line seems to be that aside from what few documents there are, and aside from newspaper accounts (and remember that news writers then had the same problems with identification that history writers have today), one is free to pick and choose what he wants to believe about many of the characters of the Old West.

There is one other thing about the demise of Cole Young that merits comment. Marshal Will Loomis was in a passenger car. He only heard shots. He did not see who fired them and he did not know why they had been fired. He only assumed that something was wrong; that a train robbery was taking place. He armed himself, stepped down from the train, picked a target and fired. It was no more than coincidence that, in the dark, he shot the outlaw he'd been hunting for weeks, although one observer has noted that Loomis had been tipped off to expect a robbery attempt. No modern peace officer would fire under similar circumstances, however, without confirming the events taking place, without knowing the identity of the target, without issuing a warning, or without being fired upon first. Times have changed and that is as it should be.

ENDNOTE:

[1] Historian Don Cline of Albuquerque believes that the name *Code* was incorrect from the beginning. Cline has never found any reference to Code Young or Estes. He believes some earlier researcher misunderstood, or misstated, the name, and subsequent writers compounded the error.

SOURCES:

Don Bullis, "The Saga of Cole Young, Train Robber," Rio Rancho *Observer*, January 4 & 25, 1989

Donald Cline, "Cole Young, Train Robber." *Old West*, Summer 1985

Dan L. Thrapp, *Encyclopedia of Frontier Biography*

Roswell, Chaves County
1901

Deputy Rainbolt Shot at Town Dance
Dies in Brother's Arms
Nathan Hendricks on the Run

Chaves County sheriff Fred Higgins was out of town at mid-February in 1901, and his chief deputy, and brother-in-law, twenty-five-year-old Will Rainbolt was in charge. The young deputy received information that one Oliver Hendricks, a young cowboy, was packing a gun at a dance being held in the southwestern part of Roswell. Accompanied by his brother, Mody, Rainbolt drove his buggy to the dance and soon located Hendricks who was engaged in a dance. The officer waited patiently until the music stopped before he approached Hendricks. Rainbolt asked the young man to give up his gun, which Hendricks did. Rainbolt then told Hendricks to get into his buggy so that he could take him to jail.

At about that time, Oliver Hendricks' brother, Nathan, appeared and attempted to talk Will Rainbolt out of arresting his younger brother. Rainbolt was not persuaded, whereupon Nathan drew his own gun

164

and shot the deputy before the officer had any chance to draw his own gun. The bullet hit Rainbolt in the right arm, passed through or near his heart, and lodged under the skin on the left side.

"They have killed me," Rainbolt said to Mody, and died.

The Hendricks brothers mounted a single horse and rode out of town, toward a cow camp at Eight Mile, west of Roswell. There they secured two fresh mounts and continued their flight, to the west. A posse soon took up pursuit of the killer, but was unsuccessful. The local newspaper said the posse's failure was due to ineffectual leadership since the sheriff was away and the chief deputy was dead.

A young wife and child, as well as his parents, survived Deputy Rainbolt. His funeral was held on Sunday, February 10, and the officer was interred at the South Side Cemetery in Roswell. The tragic affair was "largely attended."

Rumors later circulated that there was more to the affair than met the eye. Some said there was bad blood between Rainbolt and the Hendricks brothers which resulted from a confrontation two years previously in which Rainbolt shot the McElroy brothers. It was said that the McElroys and the Hendricks' were friends and the Hendricks brothers had gone about armed for the purpose of settling the score with Rainbolt at the best opportunity.

Sheriff Higgins returned to Roswell in time for his deputy's funeral, and began a pursuit of the killer, but it was too late. Higgins was able to trace Nathan Hendricks several years later, and returned him to Roswell for trial. Hendricks was first tried in 1903. He claimed that he shot Rainbolt in defense of his brother's life. He was convicted of third-degree murder and sentenced to eight years in prison. An appeals court remanded the case to Chaves County on the basis of incorrect jury instructions. After a second trial in 1906, Hendricks was found not guilty of murder. He was released and returned to his new home in South Dakota.

The local newspaper editorialized thus:

> The tragic death of Deputy Sheriff Will Rainbolt is another proof that heavy fines for carrying concealed

weapons are not entirely successful in preventing the practice. In the absence of something better it would be a good thing to make the fine an even $100 and see how that would work. The time has long passed in this country when it is necessary for anybody to go armed, and as long as they do, murder is at our elbow all the time. The pernicious habit of carrying a gun is responsible for more murders than either whiskey or women, the two great prompters of crime.

SOURCES:

Roswell *Record*, February 15, 1901
Roswell *Daily Record*, June 2 & August 4, 2000
Cecil Bonney, *Looking Over My Shoulder: Seventy-five years in the Pecos Valley*
Elvis Fleming, Historian, City of Roswell, correspondence, December 9, 1999, January 7, 2000

Santa Fe Plaza, Santa Fe County
1854

Duel Claims "The Skimmer of the Plains"
Aubry's Pistol No Match for
Weightman's Bowie Knife

When two determined and prideful men fall into dispute, the results can be devastating, and that was the case when Francis X. Aubry, known as the "Skimmer of the Plains," and Richard H. Weightman, a political figure and newspaperman, met in a Santa Fe saloon in August 1854.

Aubry, a French Canadian born in 1824, acquired his sobriquet by breaking all speed records for travel between Santa Fe and Independence, Missouri. His first record was 14 days; his second eight days and 10 hours; and his third and final was five days and 16 hours. Here is what one historian said about his ride: ... "[he] broke down six horses, walked 20 miles afoot, slept only two and one-half hours, ate but six meals, endured a 24 hour rain, traveled nearly 600 miles through mud, and made one 190 mile stretch in 24 hours." Exciting stuff. Aubry's record stands to this day, and is not likely to be broken.

General Richard Hanson Weightman (top left), Francois Xavier Aubry (top right), and Chief Justice Joab Houghton (bottom). After Twitchell.

168

He earned his living as a trader over the Santa Fe Trail, and he was a trendsetter in that endeavor, too. He was the first of the Santa Fe merchants to make two round trips between New Mexico and Missouri in the same year. He was also among such notables at Kit Carson, Richens "Uncle Dick" Wootton and J. Francisco Chaves in driving sheep from New Mexico west to California where they were sold for a good profit. He made his home in Santa Fe where he had many friends.

Richard H. Weightman was a native of Washington, D. C. born in 1816. One historian says he was educated at West Point, but another reports that he was expelled from the military academy for engaging in a knife fight. By the late 1840's he was living in St. Louis, and when the call went out for fighting men to join Colonel Stephen Watts Kearny and his "Army of the West" early in the Mexican War, Weightman signed up. He saw combat in Mexico and attained the rank of Major by war's end. He settled in Santa Fe by 1849 where he practiced law and involved himself in politics, and, for a time, he published a newspaper called *Amigo del Pais*. In a short time he earned a reputation as "a gentleman with a temper."

His first duel was with Territorial Supreme Court Justice Joab Houghton. It didn't amount to much. At the appointed time and place, the two men observed the decorum of the affair of honor, and Weightman fired first, and missed. Houghton claimed he never heard the command to fire, and therefore did not. No blood was shed and the matter was apparently resolved.

That would not be the case in the fight with Aubry.

Witnesses in court proceedings reported on the affair. On August 18, 1854, Aubry returned to Santa Fe from a jaunt to California. He tied up his horse and entered the Mercure Brothers store — which also served as a saloon — on the south side of the plaza. Weightman saw Aubry enter the store and remarked to a friend that he "must go to see him." The two of them began an amiable conversation, during which Aubry offered Weightman a drink. Weightman declined. The chat turned to *Amigo del Pais*, and Aubry asked the former publisher what had become of his newspaper. Weightman replied that it had "died for want of subscribers." Aubry said words to the effect that any such lying paper ought to die. Weightman demanded to know what Aubry was talking about, and Aubry replied that the newspaper had "abused" him. Weightman replied that it was not so. Aubry slammed his fist down on the bar and declared, "I say it is so!" Where upon Weightman picked up a drink glass and threw the contents into Aubry's face and stepped back a couple of steps, putting hands on his belt. Aubry, for his part, drew a "five-shooter" but fired prematurely, the bullet going into the ceiling. Weightman quickly drew his Bowie knife and then grasped his foe before he could level the gun for a second shot. He plunged the knife into Aubry's stomach. The Skimmer of the Plains was dead in about 10 minutes.

Weightman was subsequently arrested by U. S. Marshal Charles Blumner and charged with murder. The matter was heard before Judge Kirby Benedict during the September term of the court, and nothing was introduced into evidence to contradict events as described above. The jury foreman, Vincente Garcia, said, "We have unanimously agreed and are of the opinion that the defendant is not guilty, because he committed such an act in defense of his person."

Thus the matter was concluded. Weightman soon left Santa Fe and returned to Missouri. When the Civil War began, he was put in command of a Confederate cavalry unit. He was killed at the battle of Wilson Creek in August 1861.

SOURCES:

Larry D. Ball, *The United States Marshals of New Mexico & Arizona Territories, 1846-1912*
R. L. Duffus, *The Santa Fe Trail*
Francis & Roberta Fugate, *Roadside History of New Mexico*
Howard Lamar, *The Far Southwest, 1846-1912*
Marc Simmons, *Albuquerque, A Narrative History*
Dan L. Thrapp, *Encyclopedia of Frontier Biography*

San Juan County

1881

The Demise of the Stockton Brothers
Two Really Bad Men — Killers & Thieves
Bite the Dust in Separate Gun Fights

There were three armed clashes in late 19th century New Mexico that came to be called "Wars:" The Colfax County War (1875-76), the Lincoln County War (1878-1881) and the San Juan County War (1881).[1] Few Old West characters can be said to have participated — to a greater or lesser degree — in all three, but Ike and Port Stockton are the exceptions.

The Stockton brothers were both born in Johnson County, Texas, Ike in 1852 and Port in 1854. Legend holds that Port killed his first man when he was only 12 years old. At 17 he shot another man and was charged with attempted murder. Ike is said to have broken Port out of jail, and the brothers fled to New Mexico, by way of Dodge City, Kansas. One source indicates that the two of them operated a saloon in the town of Lincoln. Another reports that the saloon was solely Ike's.

171

Discrepancies like this may be the reason so little has been written about the Stockton brothers. For instance, one source says that Port murdered a man named Antonio Archbie in Colfax County in January 1876. No other source mentions this killing. It is documented, however, that in October 1876, Port got into an argument with one Juan Gonzales in the town of Cimarron, in Colfax County. The Texan drew his pistol and killed Gonzales. Gonzales was not armed and Port was jailed.

One source says that Ike came to the rescue again, and helped Port escape to Trinidad, Colorado. Later the same month, Port was captured by the sheriff of Conejos County and promptly returned to New Mexico. Sketchy sources report that the younger Stockton was acquitted upon a plea of self-defense. Nothing explains how that could be, since Gonzales was unarmed.

What is known for sure is that in December Port murdered another man in Trinidad after an argument over a card game. His victim was, again, unarmed. And, for a third time, Ike engineered an escape from jail. Again, sources are not clear. Ike may have been with Port up to this time, and have gone to Lincoln in late 1876 when Port moved on to Animas City, Colorado, near the present Durango.

In Animas City, Port served a short time as town marshal. While getting a shave one day, the barber, a Black man, accidentally nicked the Texan. Port pulled his gun and chased the man down the street, shooting as they ran. Local folks took a dim view of the altercation. Port was not only fired from his job as marshal, but run out of town. He then went to Lincoln, New Mexico—by way of Rico, Colorado—and rejoined Ike.

At some point along the way, Port married and fathered two daughters.

Exactly where Port was in 1878-79 is unclear, but he may have gone back to northeastern New Mexico. One source says he killed a man named Ed Withers at Otero in June of 1879.

Brother Ike was definitely in the town of Lincoln, New Mexico on April 1, 1878. When William Bonney—Billy the Kid—and seven or eight other cowards shot Sheriff William Brady and Deputy George

172

Hindman from ambush on that date, it was saloonkeeper Ike Stockton who ran into the street to help Hindman, only to be driven off by rifle fire. By later the same year, both of the Stockton brothers are known to have been in northwest New Mexico/southwest Colorado. Port lived near Aztec and Ike at Durango. Both were active in cattle rustling and assorted other criminal activity, but it does not appear that they necessarily worked their thievery together.

Port ran with two other undesirables named Harge Eskridge and Jim Garret. On New Year's Eve, 1880, the three of them got drunk at a party, and were ejected. They returned and shot up the place. One source says that hard feelings from this event marked the beginning of the end for Port Stockton.

Again, reports on the event don't agree. One says that on January 10, 1881, a rancher named Alfred Graves tracked some stolen cattle to Port's ranch, and in the gunfight that followed, Port was killed. Another says that Graves and Stockton had a "difference of opinion" and as Graves rode past Port's house, Port grabbed a rifle and yelled for Graves to come back and talk. Graves dismounted and walked up to the rustler. He put five bullets into Port before Port could put even one into him. Both sources agree that Port's wife, Irma, grabbed a gun and took a shot at her husband's assailant. Graves is said to have placed a shot into a wagon spoke near Irma's head, which drove splinters into her face and eyes, ending the fight.

Some believe Port's killing touched off the San Juan County War, inasmuch as Ike swore revenge upon those who'd killed his brother. Ike stepped up his rustling activities, and is said to have killed at least one New Mexico rancher, Aaron Barker, in March of 1881.

On April 11, a "posse" of New Mexico ranchers—among them Alfred Graves—cowboys and gun hands invaded Durango for the avowed purpose of ridding the region of rustlers led by Ike Stockton. What followed became largely a fiasco. The New Mexicans took a position on a *mesa* overlooking Durango and the firing commenced on April 12th. Each side fired hundreds of shots, but when the smoke cleared, no one had been killed, and the New Mexicans withdrew.

Ike seems to have got the point, though, and shifted his attention to stagecoach robbery. Even so, his days were numbered. New Mexico Governor Lew Wallace posted a reward for his arrest in the amount of $2,250. One of Ike's cohorts, Burt Wilkinson, was captured and promptly lynched at Silverton, Colorado, in August. Another, Bud Galbreth, was arrested and charged with murder, rape, arson and stock stealing in September. Sheriff Barney Watson went looking for Ike. On September 26, 1881, he found him, on a street in Durango. In the gunfight that followed, Ike took a bullet in the leg (one source says the knee, another the thigh) and was captured. Doctors determined that amputation was necessary and went to work cutting off a sizable portion of his leg. Ike would not have to suffer life as a one-legged man, though, because he died the next day from loss of blood.

Thus ended the careers of the Stockton brothers, neither of whom had reached the age of 30. Western historian Ramon Adams said this: "[Ike and Port were] bad men of the first order."

ENDNOTE:

1 An incident of violence in Lincoln County in the early 1870s is sometimes called the Horrell War, but it wasn't a war in the sense the other three were.

SOURCES:

Larry D. Ball, *Desert Lawmen*
Fred M. Johnson, "When New Mexico Invaded Colorado," *True West*, January 1992
Bill O'Neal, *Encyclopedia of Western Gunfighters*
Marc Simmons, *When Six-Guns Ruled*
Dan L. Thrapp, *Encyclopedia of Frontier Biography*
Robert M. Utley, *High Noon in Lincoln*

Silver City Area, Grant County
1884

Joy Gang Kills Trainman in Robbery
Captured & Escaped
Escaped Again – All Hanged but Joy

A headline and story in the Albuquerque *Morning Journal* for March 11, 1884 read:

WILL ROB NO MORE
– – – –
The Whole Gang of Train Robbers Bite the Dust
– – – – –

Mitch Lee, Kit Joy, Frank Taggart
And Geo. Cleveland Gone Where
The Woodbine Twineth and
The Wicked Cease from
Troubling

Silver City, N. M., March 10—Four of the train robbers and Carlos Chávez, the murderer and Charles Spencer, the horse thief…broke jail this morning at 9 o'clock. A large posse of our citizens immediately followed them to the foothills of the Pinos Altos range which is some six miles north of town, where they overtook them, and in the desperate fight that ensued one of our most estimable citizens, J. W. Laffer[1] was killed, as was also George W. Cleveland, the negro [sic] train robber, and Carlos Chávez, the murderer of the Chinaman at Fort Bayard, Mitch Lee was wounded and captured and Frank Taggart was also captured. Both of these men were hung one half mile from where they were captured by a party of determined citizens. Kit Joy, another of the train robbers, is still at large. He is the man who murdered Joseph W. Laffer…. A party of three started in pursuit of Joy, and it is believed that he was overtaken and killed as his pursuers are very reticent about the matter. In any event, he is badly wounded and his escape is simply impossible.

John W. Laffer[1] [sic] was one of our foremost and most enterprising businessmen, esteemed by all who knew him and that he should meet his death at the hands of such a gang seems almost unbearable.

The negro Cleveland was captured by Sheriff Whitehill and brought here by Socorro county officers, he is the man who gave the officers a clue by which all the others have been arrested. Taggert is the man captured near St. John, [sic] Arizona, and brought back here via Albuquerque by Sheriff Whitehill and his son. Mitch Lee was taken in the American Valley country not a great while ago while Kit Joy has only been in custody a short time.

176

This is the gang that threw the Southern Pacific train off the track at Deming, and then shot the engineer. This death for the desperadoes is a fitting one and nobody in the Territory will regret the fact that they are gone never to return. There seems to be no doubt, but what Kit Joy has gone beyond.

Christopher "Kit" Joy may have been born in Texas about 1860, but his parents and a sister lived at Hillsboro, New Mexico in the middle 1880s. He is known to have spent some time around Tombstone, Arizona before he arrived in the Silver City, New Mexico, area where he worked as a cowboy. One of his employers was none other than Sheriff Harvey Whitehill. One reporter said that Joy rode with Billy the Kid at one time, and while they would have been about the same age, sources consulted do not support the contention.

The train robbery mentioned above took place on November 24, 1883 at Gage, New Mexico, about 15 miles west of Deming. The robbers were Kit Joy, Mitch Lee, Frank Taggart—all cowboys—and George Cleveland. Mitch Lee shot and killed engineer Theopholus C. Webster after the train was derailed. Investigators located the bandits' camp nearby. The outlaws had fled, but they left behind a recent edition of a California newspaper.[2] The detectives located a Silver City saloonkeeper who hailed from California and subscribed to the paper. While he had no specific recollection of that particular issue, the officers became convinced the robbers were from Silver City.

Further investigation led officers to Frank Taggart, and he was known to associate with the other three men. Whitehill learned that Cleveland was in Socorro, and arrested him in a hotel there. By means of a ruse, he got Cleveland to confirm the identities of his companions. Kit Joy and Mitch Lee were captured by ranchers near Horse Springs, New Mexico in January 1884. Taggart was captured in Apache County, Arizona the same month. All were jailed at Silver City.

And they all escaped on March 10, taking Charlie Spencer and Carlos Chávez with them. One source reports that the posse overtook the outlaws about three miles north of Silver City, and a running gunfight developed from there, which covered some five miles. During this time, Cleveland and Chávez were killed. Some believe that the posse did not kill Cleveland, but that Kit Joy, or one of the other train robbers, did the deed in revenge for Cleveland's cooperation with Sheriff Whitehill.

So the tally for the day was one posseman, Joseph Laffer, dead; four outlaws dead — two shot (Chávez and Cleveland) and two hanged (Lee and Taggart); and one escapee (Kit Joy). Only Charlie Spencer was returned to jail that evening. And contrary to the wishful thinking displayed by the writer of the above news item, Kit Joy was not wounded or killed by his pursuers, or soon captured. One source, many years after the fact, indicates that the hanging of Frank Taggart was "unjust".

Joy managed to get to the Gila River country in northern Grant County, where he stole food to survive. A group of local ranchers formed an *ad hoc* posse for the purpose of capturing the outlaw. On the morning of March 21, the searchers spotted Joy. Rancher Erichus "Rackety" Smith opened fire. His second shot took the outlaw in the left leg, just below the knee. The wound required amputation of the limb. Joy was tried at Hillsboro in November 1884 for the murder of railroad engineer T. C. Webster. Convicted of second-degree murder, he was sentenced to life in prison. He was released some years later and retired to Bisbee, Arizona. He was never tried for killing Joseph Laffer.

Harvey Whitehill was one of the better-known peace officers in Territorial New Mexico, but he was not Grant County sheriff when these events took place, even though he did participate in them.[3] He was elected sheriff in 1874 and served until 1882 when he was elected to the Territorial legislature. He served a final term as sheriff in 1889-90. He is probably best known for being the first lawman to arrest William H. Bonney, aka Billy the Kid, for petty thievery, in 1875; but he was involved in many adventures as a peace officer. Sheriff Whitehill died at Deming in 1906 at the age of 69. He was buried at Silver City.

ENDNOTES:

[1] Another source identifies this citizen as Joseph N. Lafferr.

[2] A second source claims the newspaper was from Kansas and the subscriber did remember who received the page from him.

[3] James B. Woods was Grant County sheriff from 1883 to 1887. Woods was active in capturing the train robbers, but he was visiting in Arkansas when the jailbreak occurred.

SOURCES:

Albuquerque *Morning Journal*, Tuesday, March 11, 1884

Bob Alexander, *Lawmen, Outlaws, and S. O. Bs*

Bob Alexander, *Sheriff Harvey Whitehill: Silver City Stalwart*

Larry D. Ball, *Desert Lawmen, The High Sheriff's of New Mexico and Arizona, 1846-1912*

Howard Bryan, "The Gage Train Robbers." *Robbers, Rogues and Ruffians*

Jay Robert Nash, *Encyclopedia of Western Lawmen & Outlaws*

Dan L. Thrapp, *Encyclopedia of Frontier Biography*

Silver City, Grant County
1895

Bullets Fly in White House Saloon
Marshal Cantley Killed While Drunk
No One Else Injured

Gunfights are part and parcel of the literature — including television and the movies — of the Old West. Such events were usually portrayed as matters of honor, or villainy, in which two men faced each other in the middle of a dusty street, drew holstered six-guns and fired at one another. Readers will recall that Marshal Matt Dillon of television's *Gunsmoke* fame only required a single shot to bring down his adversary at the opening of each show. So did Roy Rogers, Gene Autry, John Wayne and many others.

The problem is that history does not record a single instance of such a fight ever taking place.[1]

What follows is an abridged account of a real-life gunfight, taken from the Silver City (New Mexico) *Enterprise* for October 11, 1895.

At twenty-five minutes past 10 o'clock on Tuesday eve-

180

ning (Oct. 8), the citizens of Silver City were startled by the loud reports of six pistol shots fired in regular and precise order of about a half-second apart, followed by an interval of a few seconds by two more shots....

The affray occurred at the White House Saloon, into which place Mr. [James] Fielder had stepped for a few moments before going home [after] simply taking a stroll through the town before retiring for the night. Walking through the club room to go out he was accosted by Marshall [*sic*] [Charles] Cantley, who had been drinking and was considerably under the influence of liquor. Their conversation at first was of a pleasant and jovial character, but soon Cantley became angry and aggressive, as he often did while drinking. Mr. Fielder strove to placate and pacify him but without avail.

Witness John Gillett described what happened then:
Cantley was drinking during the evening and Mr. Harvey, myself, and others had been trying to get him home for an hour and a half but could not. I had been in the back room a short time when I heard the words uttered by Mr. Fielder, 'liar or damned liar.' I stepped out of the back room and walked up and stood by Mr. Cantley. Mr. Cantley said to Mr. Fielder, 'I've been told that you said you were going to beat the stuffing out of me.' Mr. Fielder said he had never said so, and that whoever told him so was a liar. After some farther parley about some lawsuit, Cantley said he had personal reasons for knowing he had it in for him. Fielder told Cantley, 'Cantley I have nothing on earth against you; I've always been your friend.' Cantley asked Mr. Fielder if he was armed. Mr. Fielder replied, 'I do not think you have any right to ask me that question.'

181

Mr. Cantley then pulled his pistol and fired; Mr. Fielder pulled his pistol and fired; his pistol apparently going off before he had it up and I think the first shot went into the floor. Then they both continued to fire. After the third or fourth shot Cantley staggered and started to fall. After Cantley fell or was falling Mr. Fielder stepped forward and fired another shot with his pistol in both hands, he then snapped his pistol once or twice more at Cantley but it was empty.

Under the heading, INCIDENTS OF THE SHOOTING, the *Enterprise* reporter provided the following details.

When Cantley pulled his gun Mr. Fielder coolly reached for his cigar and placed it in the other side of his mouth, at the same time freeing his elbows from the place they occupied between the pickets of the railing against which he was standing, and stepped to one side of the railing so that his arms were unobstructed.

From the relative positions of the combatants and the bullet marks in the wall behind where Mr. Fielder stood, it is evident that each of the bullets fired from Mr. Cantley's pistol only missed his opponent by a few inches. One bullet went too high and to the left of Mr. Fielder's head, one just to the right of his breast. Mr. Fielder's first shot evidently went into the floor between them, his second evidently struck the deceased above and outward of the nipple of the left breast, another struck him in the neck above the left clavicle, when he commenced to stagger and fall, and another after he had fallen grazed his chin on the left side, going downward through the neck into the body. One of the bullets fired by Mr. Fielder went over his antagonist's head and bedded itself in the wall. Mr. Fielder testified that after the

182

first shot was fired by Cantley he could not see him on account of the [gun] smoke, and he just fired at the point where the flashes were coming from, until Cantley fell.

Charley Cantley, a native of Anderson County, Texas, had resided in Silver City for about 10 years at the time of his death, and had served as a lawman for the entire period, first as a deputy sheriff and then as city marshal. He was well regarded and generally considered fearless in the face of the outlaw element. The *Enterprise*, though, said this: "His long continued authority as an officer … had caused him to assume an arbitrary demeanor, which at times tended toward aggressiveness. Liquor, to which he was slightly addicted, would aggravate this tendency…

The business houses in the city all closed during the funeral which was largely attended by all of our best citizens.

Justice of the Peace Isaac Givens ruled the case a matter of self-defense, and the *Enterprise* concluded thus:
The whole affair is to be deplored.

ENDNOTE:

[1] The closest was probably the fight between James Butler "Wild Bill" Hickok and Dave Tutt in Springfield, Missouri on June 21, 1865. At a range of 75 to 100 yards, they both drew their guns at about the same time and began firing. Hickok made what had to be a lucky shot at that range and killed Tutt with a bullet to the heart.

SOURCE:

Thanks to Historian Terry Humble of Silver City for the clippings.

Silver City, Grant County
1904

Drunken Cowboy Shoots, Kills
Marshal Kilburn & Constable Rodríguez
Killer Shot, Captured & Jailed — Escapes the Noose

The story began when five cowboys from the Victorio Land and Cattle Company rode into Silver City, New Mexico, on Saturday afternoon, August 27, 1904. Another source says there were just three of them. Fall roundup was scheduled to begin the following week and there would be no opportunity to get back to town until the work was done. Drinking in the Club House and Palace Saloons was the order of the day and two of the cowboys, Howard Chenowth and Mart Kennedy far overdid it. At one point during the evening, the two engaged in a loud quarrel along a city street and Victorio ranch foreman Pat Nunn intervened. And before August 27th became August 28th, Chenowth tried to ride his horse into the Palace Saloon, only to be stopped by Nunn and Deputy Sheriff Elmore Murray.

It was close to two o'clock on the morning of the 28th when Nunn and Murray encountered the two cowboys on the street. One version of the story goes that Chenowth and Kennedy were fighting and Nunn interceded. Another version holds that Nunn simply told the two men to return to the ranch because both were drunk. Chenowth agreed to go and mounted his horse. Kennedy, angered at being ordered to cease his revelry, refused to go. He said he'd quit the Victorio and he took his saddle off the company horse. He called Nunn an "ugly" name. The ranch foreman resented the remark (whatever it was), dismounted his horse, removed his gunbelt and placed it on the curb before he engaged Kennedy in a fistfight.

The fight didn't last long. Nunn was a bigger man, physically, and he was sober. He knocked the cowboy to the ground and stood over him as Chenowth removed Nunn's gun from its holster and announced that he would not allow anyone to harm his friend. Chenowth fired. The first bullet hit Nunn in the chest, exactly where he carried a watch in his shirt pocket. The timepiece was ruined but Nunn was not otherwise injured. The second bullet grazed the foreman's forehead removing both eyebrows.

Deputy Murray struggled to get the gun away from Chenowth. An elderly man named H. A. McGowan tried to help the deputy as Precinct Constable Perfecto Rodríguez approached the scene. He'd been visiting a nearby saloon, heard the shots and ran into the street to learn the cause of the disturbance.

"Get the gun!" he yelled at Murray.

"That is just what I am trying to do," the deputy responded just as Chenowth shot the constable in the chest, knocking him down.

Chenowth broke free and he and Kennedy fled north on Texas Street with Deputy Murray close at hand, still trying to get Nunn's gun away from Chenowth and trying to prevent Kennedy from drawing his own gun. Sources at the time reported that Deputy Murray had been friendly with the two cowboys, which may account for the fact that they didn't shoot him.

Town Marshal William Kilburn, who lived only two blocks away, hurried to the scene and came upon the three men. Murray told Kilburn to get Chenowth's gun, but before the marshal could take any action, Che-

185

nowth shot the lawman in the neck, rendering him immediately unconscious. The two cowboys broke away again and fled the scene on foot.

A sizable crowd gathered. Constable Rodríguez was found to be dead from his wound and Marshal Kilburn, severely wounded, was removed to Ladies' Hospital. He was not expected to survive. Neither of the two lawmen had been armed. Officers and citizens soon developed a plan to search Silver City for the killers. About then, Mart Kennedy walked into the Palace Saloon and ordered a drink. He announced that he'd done nothing wrong and shouldn't be arrested. He was quickly taken into custody. A Justice of the Peace had already issued murder warrants for both of the offending cowboys.

A jailer named Gill and three deputies, Charles Williams, John Burnside and John Collier, escorted Kennedy to jail, keeping a careful lookout for Chenowth. As the party passed Samuel Lindaner's dry goods store, Collier spotted Chenowth hiding behind some boxes on the sidewalk. He said nothing for some distance and then told Burnside. The group shortly encountered a citizen who provided Collier with a shotgun. Unfortunately, it was not loaded and the deputy was obliged to return to the Club House Saloon for ammunition. Then he moved carefully along the street until he stood in front of Lindaner's store, in the middle of the street.

Collier ordered Chenowth to surrender, several times, and Chenowth refused every time. At Burnside's warning, Collier took cover behind a tree in front of the Silver City Mercantile. Collier again ordered Chenowth to give up. Chenowth refused and advanced toward Collier, gun in hand. The cowboy stopped behind a signpost and started to take aim at the deputy, and as he did, Collier fired. Half a load of number six birdshot splintered the post and the other half hit Chenowth in the side of the head. It didn't kill him but he went down immediately and was arrested.[1]

Constable Rodríguez, 45, was well known in Grant County and Southern New Mexico as he had been active in politics for many years. He'd previously served as Deputy U. S. Marshal in addition to several terms as constable. A wife and six children survived him. The local newspaper said, "...[his] remains were followed to their last resting place by a large number of friends."

Marshal Kilburn, 40, died of his wound a week later. He was born in Missouri but spent most of his adult life in Colorado and New Mexico. Kilburn served as a Grant County deputy under Sheriff Harvey Whitehill[2] before becoming Silver City Town Marshal in 1888. He served until 1891 and was re-elected to the post in 1895 and again in 1903. His wife, Emma, was Whitehill's daughter. Kilburn left four children behind. The local paper said this about Marshal William Kilburn: "As a peace officer he was especially gifted. He was absolutely fearless in the discharge of his duties and at the same time exercised such good sense and judgment that even those whom he was compelled to exert his authority upon were his friends."

Chenowth was tried and convicted of first-degree murder of both Kilburn and Rodríguez. He had, after all, pulled the trigger in both cases. Judge Frank Parker sentenced him to 50 years in prison. With the help of his family, however, he escaped from the Grant County jail on Christmas day, 1905. He reportedly fled to Brazil where he worked for some years as a cowboy. He also married and fathered seven children. In 1927, through the efforts of his family, New Mexico Governor Richard C. Dillon pardoned Howard Chenowth. The governor said the crime had been "the act of an irresponsible youth under the influence of alcohol." (Never mind that Perfecto Rodríguez's six children grew up without their father because of the *irresponsible youth*; and never mind that Chenowth never paid for his crime.) The killer died in 1947.

ENDNOTES:

[1] Another version of the story, which appeared in an Albuquerque newspaper, was that Deputy Murray shot Chenowth. The above retelling is based on detailed accounts reported in the Silver City newspapers of the day.

[2] Grant County Sheriff Harvey Whitehill was the first lawman to arrest William Bonney — Billy the Kid — for stealing butter, in 1875.

SOURCES:

Bob Alexander, *Lawmen, Outlaws, and S. O. Bs*

Albuquerque *Morning Journal*, August 29, 1904

Robert Mullin, *A Chronology of The Lincoln County War*. New Mexico Historical Review, 1957-58

Silver City *Independent*, August 30, September 6 & 9, 1904

Chief Thomas J. Ryan (Ret.), Silver City Police Department, correspondence, October 2 & 23, 1991

Stinking Spring, McKinley County
1937

FBI Agent Truett Rowe Falls To Bandit's Gun
Local Officers Arrest Killer Osborne
Short Stirrups Gave Him Away

The warden of the Oklahoma State Prison at McAlester described George Guy "Bud" Osborne as "a punk, a louse, a habitual liar and absolutely unreliable." Osborne was released from the Oklahoma Prison in October, 1936 and arrested again in the spring of 1937 at Eufala, Oklahoma, for auto theft. He soon escaped from jail and made his way to Pampa, Texas, where he stole a car and headed toward New Mexico. Because his criminal activities took him across state lines, Osborne became of interest to the Federal Bureau of Investigation.

Special Agent Truett E. Rowe, 33, worked out of the FBI's El Paso Field Office (which at the time took in all of New Mexico). In late May, 1937, Rowe learned that Bud Osborne had a brother, Wes Osborne, living near Gallup. The agent took a bus to Albuquerque and then another one to Gallup.

On June 1st, Rowe walked into the office of Gallup Police Chief

189

FBI Agent Truett Rowe

Kelsey Pressley and asked for a ride out to the Osborne place. Pressley didn't know where Osborne lived and suggested the agent try the Sheriff's Department. Rowe learned that Sheriff Dee Roberts was away from the office, fishing near Ramah. He returned to the police department and Chief Pressley agreed to drive the federal officer.

After asking around, Pressley learned that Osborne's small ranch was near Stinking Spring, 17, or so, miles south of town. The chief found it with no trouble. Wes Osborne, his wife Ethel, and 13-year-old son, J. W., greeted the officers in the door yard as Bud Osborne fled from the house to the barn. Young J. W. went into the barn and told his uncle that Chief Pressley was outside with a man in a gray suit. Bud and his nephew walked out of the barn. Agent Rowe identified himself and asked the suspect to go to Gallup for questioning. Bud Osborne agreed but asked to be allowed to change clothes and pack some things. Rowe agreed and followed the ex-con into a bedroom in the small clapboard house. Chief Pressley kept an eye on other members of the family, including Bud's 17-year-old wife, Betsy Louise. Pressley heard a shot and Bud Osborne suddenly appeared in the doorway, a gun, a .32-caliber revolver, in his hand. The chief drew his own gun but it misfired and Osborne fled out the back door and disappeared into some brush.

Agent Rowe made it to the yard in front of the house where he dropped to his hands and knees. He was losing a lot of blood. He asked the chief to get him to a hospital as soon as possible. Pressley and Wes Osborne got the agent into the car and Pressley headed for Gallup.

190

Later the chief recalled hearing the agent plead: "Open the door and give me some air! For God's sake, chief, give me some air!"

Pressley said all the windows were rolled down in his car and he was driving 80 miles per hour. At St. Mary's Hospital, Sister Mary Carina, a nurse, declared the agent dead.

After he fled the house, Bud Osborne doubled back and took J. W.'s horse which was saddled and standing near the barn. He mounted up and headed for a bluff called The Hogback west of Stinking Springs.

Undersheriff Dwight Craig heard news of the shooting. He recruited three Navajo trackers and along with Deputy Sheriff Edison "Bobcat" Wilson he headed for Stinking Spring in pursuit of the killer. They picked up Bud's trail and were following it when Chief Pressley and Assistant Police Chief Les Mahoney arrived back at Wes Osborne's house. The chief saw a rider herding cows along an *arroyo* and coming toward the house. Pressley, himself a cattleman, noticed that the drover's stirrups seemed to be much too short, and they were; they'd been adjusted for use by Osborne's 13-year-old nephew. The officers quickly drove their cars into the small herd and Assistant Chief Mahoney pulled down on the rider with a shotgun.

"You aren't as smart as you thought you were," Pressley said.

"No, but I damn near got away with it," Osborne said.

Federal Agents from El Paso, St. Louis and Kansas City converged on Gallup. They transferred Osborne from the McKinley County Jail to Albuquerque. At his trial in September, Osborne claimed the shooting was an accident. He said he'd dropped the gun as he and Rowe struggled, and it accidentally discharged. The jury didn't buy it and on September 30, 1937, Bud Osborne was convicted of first-degree murder. He was sentenced to life in prison but was released in the late 1960s. Bud Osborne died in Dallas in 1975, thirty-eight years after he killed Truett Rowe.

Agent Rowe was born at Amity, Arkansas, and educated in Oklahoma City and Houston, Texas. He served in the Army and with the Border Patrol before he applied to the FBI in 1934. Famed FBI agent Melvin Purvis (the man who led the hunt for John Dillinger, Pretty

Boy Floyd, and others) wrote on Rowe's application: "Applicant has a natural investigative ability. [He is] a sharpshooter who is familiar with dangerous situations. He is all right in that respect." The FBI accepted Rowe in 1935.

On the day he died, Truett Rowe carried in his pockets and on his person an eighty-cent round-trip train ticket between Albuquerque and Gallup, $8.49 cents in cash and a loaded .38-caliber Colt revolver.

Agent Rowe was survived by his wife, Victoria. She received two checks from FBI Director J. Edgar Hoover: one for about $1,000 and a second for about $5,000. The money came from a fund made up of voluntary contributions by the 634 agents who made up the FBI in 1937. She also got a job as a secretary with the FBI field office in Chicago. Hoover said Agent Rowe's death was an "...irreplaceable loss of a devoted public servant." The agent was buried at Oklahoma City.

The FBI was created in 1908. Truett Rowe was the ninth agent killed in the line of duty, and the only FBI agent killed in New Mexico.

SOURCES:

Albuquerque *Journal*, June 2, 3, & 4; September 28, 29 & 30, 1937

Clovis *News-Journal*, June 6, 1937

Tom Kneir, Special Agent in Charge, FBI Albuquerque, correspondence, November 7, 1995

James W. Nelson, Special Agent in Charge, FBI Albuquerque, correspondence, October 24 and November 17, 1989

Bart Ripp, "The day that Truett Rowe was shot," Albuquerque *Tribune*, May 25, 1987

Turkey Canyon, Colfax County
1899

Gunfight in the Rain Near Cimarron
Sheriff Killed, Local Cowboy Wounded, Dies
Outlaw Sam Ketchum Captured – Arm Amputated

At about 10:30 on the evening of July 11, 1899, a gang of bandits made up of Sam Ketchum,[1] Harvey Logan and Elza Lay stopped the Colorado and Southern passenger train near two cinder cones called Twin Mountain, about five miles south of Folsom in Union County, New Mexico. Train Number 1 was on its regular run from Denver to Fort Worth. The thieves blew the safe in the express car and made good their escape. The railroad claimed the thieves got nothing, but other accounts at the time reported that the thieves made off with about $70,000. Logan and Lay were both regular members of Butch Cassidy's Wild Bunch, but Cassidy did not participate in the Twin Mountain robbery.

W. H. Reno, a special agent for the railroad, accompanied by Sheriff Ed Farr of Huerfano County, Colorado, soon arrived in Cimarron, New Mexico. On Sunday, July 16, officers learned that three men who

Sam Ketchum

fit the descriptions of the robbers had been seen entering Turkey Canyon, about eight miles north of Cimarron. Reno and Farr organized a posse that included Henry N. Love and Perfecto Cordova of Springer, F. H. Smith of New York (who went along for "the fun of it"), and others.[2] At about 5:15 that afternoon, the posse came upon the outlaw camp.

Bullets began flying at once. Lay was hit first but remained able to return fire. Ketchum, hit in the arm, was put out of action. Logan laid down a withering fire on the lawmen. Sheriff Farr took a bullet in the wrist. He calmly bandaged the wound with his handkerchief and continued the fight. Smith was hit in the calf of his leg and Farr was hit again, this time in the chest. He fell on top of Smith. "I'm done for," he said, and died. Love was badly wounded in the thigh. Firing died down, then. It was nearly 6:00 p.m. and beginning to rain. Early news reports indicated that one of the bandits had been killed in the fight, but that was in error. The posse remained in Turkey Canyon throughout the rainy night as all three outlaws managed to escape.[3]

Sam Ketchum, his upper arm badly shattered by a bullet, made it to the Ute Creek headquarters of the Lambert ranch, about three miles west of Turkey Canyon. Ketchum told cowboys there he'd been shot in a hunting accident. They had not heard of the gun battle and believed him. A ranch hand in Cimarron for supplies the next day learned of the gunfight and told authorities that a wounded man had appeared at the ranch. W. H. Reno and others arrested Ketchum later that day without incident. Transferred to the Territorial Prison at Santa Fe, Ketchum died of blood poisoning on July 24, 1899.

Logan and Lay rode all night and all the next day putting as much distance between themselves and Turkey Canyon as possible. Large posses searched the mountains for the outlaws, but they were hampered by almost continuous rain. One source says Logan left Lay with a man named Red Weaver who nursed the outlaw back to health. Another source says Logan paid a young Hispanic family a large sum of money to minister to Lay's wounds. Whichever it was, Lay recovered and joined Logan at the Virgil Lusk Ranch, near Eddy (now Carlsbad), in mid-August.

Lusk managed to get word to Eddy County Sheriff Miles Cicero Stewart that the outlaws were at his place. The sheriff and two deputies, J. D. Cantrell and Rufus Thomas, hurried to the ranch. In a brief gunfight, Lusk, Thomas and Lay were all wounded and Lay was captured. Under the name McGinnis, Lay was convicted of second-degree murder and sentenced to life in prison for killing Sheriff Farr. On July 1, 1905, Governor Miguel A. Otero commuted the sentence to 10 years. Elza Lay was released on January 10, 1906.[4]

Harvey Logan, also known as Kid Curry, was considered one of the most violent members of the Wild Bunch. He was never prosecuted for the murder of Sheriff Farr although he was arrested in Knoxville, Tennessee in 1901. He escaped from jail there and made his way back to the West. Logan committed suicide in July 1903, near Glenwood Springs, Colorado, after a train robbery near Parachute, rather than submit to arrest.

Posseman Henry Love died of his wound on July 20, 1899.[5]

Edward Farr was born at Kerrville, Texas and moved first to New Mexico, and then Walsenburg, Colorado, about 1887. He was elected sheriff of Huerfano County in 1898. A special train took his body from Trinidad to Walsenburg for burial on July 20, 1899.

ENDNOTES:

[1] Sam Ketchum, about 45, was the older brother of Tom Ketchum who was one of several New Mexico outlaws who used the name "Black Jack."

[2] Different sources include different posse members. One source says Deputy U. S. Marshal Wilson Elliott was a part of the posse, and in fact led it. Two other sources fail to list Elliott as a posse member. Two sources list Miguel Lopez and a Captain Thacker as posse members, while a third omits them. One source says the posse was seven men strong, another says eight. The first news reports named six possemen. Some writers seem to confuse the posse that fought in Turkey Canyon with posses that took up pursuit of the bandits afterwards.

[3] There arose a dispute after the battle as to who did what. U. S. Marshal Creighton Foraker claimed that deputy marshal Elliott was in charge at Turkey Canyon. Other reports said that Sheriff Farr had discretionary authority, and W. H. Reno claimed he was personally in charge. The fight got so acrimonious that Foraker claimed that Reno deserted the posse when the first shots were fired. There were also hard feelings because Sheriff Farr's body remained at Turkey Canyon, in the rain, overnight.

[4] The story goes that McGinnis (Elsa Lay) helped foil two escape attempts, one in 1900 and one several years later. In gratitude, Governor Miguel Otero reduced his sentence to 10 years in 1905. He remained an upright citizen after his release.

[5] The bullet that hit Love in the thigh also smashed his pocketknife, driving its blade into his leg. The knife had been used to treat cattle sick with blackleg, a form of anthrax, and it infected the cowboy with the disease which killed him four days later.

SOURCES:

Howard Bryan, "The Black Jack Gangs: The Ketchum Brothers," *Robbers, Rogues and Ruffians, True Tales of the Wild West*

Don Bullis, *New Mexico's Finest: Peace Officers Killed in the Line of Duty, 1847-1999*

Charles Kelly, *The Outlaw Trail, A History of Butch Cassidy and His Wild Bunch*

Bill O'Neal, *Encyclopedia of Western Gunfighters*

Miguel A. Otero, *My Nine Years As Governor of the Territory of New Mexico, 1897-1906*

Santa Fe *New Mexican*, July 12, 17, 18, 19, 20, 21 & 25; August 16, 1899

Dan L. Thrapp, *Encyclopedia of Frontier Biography*

White Oaks, Lincoln County
1878

Outlaws Shoot Up Town, Target Deputy Redman
Blacksmith J. Carlyle Killed at Greathouse Tavern
Former Liveryman, B. Wilson, With Outlaws

Billy Wilson was born in Trumbull County, in far northeastern Ohio, in 1861[1]. Along with his family, he moved to West Texas, probably in the 1870s. By the time he was 18, he operated at livery stable at White Oaks, Lincoln County, New Mexico. He sold out a year later to a man named West who paid him with four one-hundred-dollar bills, or so he alleged. He rode over to the town of Lincoln where he made some purchases from merchant Jimmy Dolan. The problem was that the hundred-dollar bill he used was counterfeit.

It is at this point that Wilson's story gets a bit murky. He did not immediately return to White Oaks to recover his property and set the matter right. If he had indeed been defrauded, one wonders why not. Instead, he rode east to the Rio Pecos country and joined up with Billy the Kid and participated in various criminal activities. It is also known that, with the gang, he visited White Oaks in late November 1880 and apparently did nothing to settle his differences with Mr. West. Federal agents at the time believed that Wilson was part of a gang which "shoved the queer," which meant putting bogus money into circulation.

While the gang, made up at that point of Wilson, Billy Bonney and Dave Rudabaugh, was in White Oaks, though, they shot up the town, in particular taking aim at a deputy sheriff named James Redman, whom they missed. A posse of townsmen pursued the outlaws to a roadside tavern known as the Kuch & Greathouse ranch.[2] It turned out that the leader of the posse, Jim Carlyle, a blacksmith, was also from Trumbull County, Ohio, and if that connection to Billy Wilson wasn't enough, it is certain that the White Oaks town blacksmith would have been acquainted with the town's livery stable operator.

Perhaps because of the relationship between the two men, Carlyle went into the tavern to arrange for surrender. What happened then is not known for sure, but later that night, for some reason, Carlyle leapt out of a window, only to be shot dead. It has never been determined for sure whether he was shot by Wilson and his friends, or by his own posse members. The outlaws escaped.

Three weeks later, on December 19, Wilson, along with Billy the Kid, Dave Rudabaugh, Charlie Bowdre, Tom O'Folliard and Tom Pickett rode into the community of Fort Sumner. Sheriff Pat Garrett had set a trap for the outlaws, and he sprung it without warning. When the fusillade was over, O'Folliard was mortally wounded and Rudabaugh's horse was dead, but the surviving outlaws escaped.

On December 23, 1880, Garrett's posse caught up with the outlaws again, this time at a place called Stinking Springs, east of Fort Sumner. Another gunfight ensued during which Charlie Bowdre was killed. Wilson, Bonney, Pickett and Rudabaugh were all captured. Wilson surrendered his recently purchased Colt .44 six-shooter to Garrett. In one of history's little ironies, this was the gun Garrett used to kill Billy the Kid less than seven months later.

Wilson was charged with counterfeiting and transported to Santa Fe for trial. In 1881, he was tried in the court of Judge Bradford Prince,

convicted and sentenced to 25 years in the Federal Prison at Leavenworth, Kansas. Historian William A. Keleher says that Wilson then followed a "time honored custom" and escaped from the Santa Fe jail.[3] It
was also in keeping with the times that he was not recaptured.

One source reports that five years later, Wilson and his old outlaw
pal, Tom Pickett, were working for the Hashknife ranch near the Little
Colorado River in northeastern Arizona. This was a time when cattle
rustling was rife, and feuding between large ranches in the area was
common. Nothing indicates that Wilson or Pickett were participants in
any of that.

Wilson moved on to Terrell County, Texas, where he assumed the
name David L. Anderson, married and fathered two children. He was
appointed a Customs Service inspector at the Langtry Port of Entry in
1891. He seems to have become a respectable member of the community. But one day in late 1895, who should happen across the international boundary but Sheriff Pat Garrett.[4] Garrett recognized the former
outlaw; and for a time Wilson/Anderson thought he would have to
serve out his prison time. Garrett, however, seems to have been im-
pressed with Wilson's turnaround in life, and the sheriff took a chance
on him.

Garrett contacted such notables as George Curry, then a Territorial
legislator, New Mexico Governor W. T. Thornton, who had served as
Wilson's attorney at his original trail 15 years before, and even Jimmy
Dolan, the recipient of Wilson's counterfeit money. They all agreed that
Wilson should probably be pardoned and his conviction vacated. Governor Thornton took the matter to President Grover Cleveland, and he
too agreed. Wilson was pardoned on July 24, 1896.

In July 1915, as D. L. Anderson, he was appointed sheriff of Terrell
County, and served until the following year. He was appointed again,
as Billie [sic] Wilson, in early 1918.[5] On June 14, 1918, Sheriff Wilson
was summoned to the railroad station in Sanderson where a young
cowboy named Ed Valentine was drunk and causing a disturbance.
Wilson was acquainted with the miscreant and didn't even arm himself to handle the matter. When he arrived at the scene, he learned that

Valentine was hiding in a baggage shed. The sheriff stepped up to the door of the structure and the cowboy shot him. Wilson soon died and a gathering of townspeople promptly lynched Ed Valentine.

One wonders if the spirit of Jim Carlyle felt avenged.

ENDNOTES:

[1] This Billy Wilson should not be confused with William J. "One-armed Billy" Wilson (1843-1920), who worked as a drover for Charles Goodnight and Oliver Loving.

[2] Some accounts of this affair suggest that this was just a normal working ranch. It was not. "Whiskey Jim" Greathouse (sometimes called Arkansas Jack) was himself an outlaw who peddled liquor to Indians and rustled cattle. He was later shot and killed for rustling.

[3] One source reports that Wilson escaped from Leavenworth Prison, but it is more probable that he escaped custody in Santa Fe.

[4] Former Territorial Governor George Curry says in his autobiography that the encounter took place at Piedras Negras, Texas, but Langtry is most likely correct.

[5] One source indicates that D. L. Anderson died while in office. That seems unlikely since Anderson and Wilson were the same person.

SOURCES:

H. B. Hening, Ed., *George Curry, 1861-1947, An Autobiography*
William A. Keleher, *Violence in Lincoln County*
Denis McLoughlin, *An Encyclopedia of the Old West*
Leon C. Metz, *Pat Garrett, The Story of a Western Lawman*
Bill O'Neal, *Encyclopedia of Western Gunfighters*
Sammy Tise, *Texas County Sheriffs*. Privately Published, limited edition

Index

202

E

Earp, Wyatt 110
Eddleston, Hugh 151-152
Eddy County 36, 92, 129
Ely, Lt. Clyde Earl 157
Emberto, Luis 51-52
Eskridge, Harge 173
Espalin, José 104, 106
Española 63
Esquibel, Solomon 82-83
Estes, Wayne 157
Evans, Jesse 141-142, 144-145
Ewell, Richard Stoddart 67

F

Fall, Albert Bacon 103
Farr, Edward 193-195
Felipe, Gabriel 9
Felipe, Willie 9
Fergusson, Harvey 134
Fernandez, Joe 9
Five Days' Battle 72, 74, 142
Fletcher, Quirino 142
Foraker, Creighton Mays 4, 196
Fornoff, Fred 31-32, 159
Fort Selden 142
Fort Stanton 67-69, 144
Fort Sumner 71-74, 87, 130, 146, 198
Fountain, Albert Jennings 38, 99,
    103-104
Fountain, Henry 107
Fowler, Joel 87
Frazier, Irvin 29-31
French, Jim 121, 123-124

G

Galbreth, Bud 174
Gallinas 6
Gallinas Springs 68
Gallup 81
Garcia, Alejandro 91
Garcia, Nash P. 8-10

Garret, Jim 173
Garrett, Patrick Floyd 27, 71, 73-74,
    86-88, 102, 104, 106, 123, 146,
    148, 198-199
Gatlin, Claude 21-23
Geronimo 13, 14
Gillett, Jim 111
Gilliland, Jim 38, 104, 106-107
Gilliland, Robert 55, 57-58
Gonzales, Willie 84
Goodman, Henry 48
Goodnight, Charles 130-131
Gragg, A. N. "Dad" 139
Grando, Francisco 31
Grant County 175, 180, 184
Grantham, Ira 89-90
Graves, Alfred 173
Graydon, James "Paddy" 67-69
Gray, Tom 37
Greathouse Ranch 85-86, 198
Greathouse, "Whiskey Jim" 87
Greer, John 29-30
Greer, Reynold 29-31
Grezelachowski, Alejandro 148
Griego, Dolores (Lola) 52
Griffin, Meade F. 33, 35
Guadalupe County 25, 146
Guerro, Vicente 12
Gutierrez, Ramon 53
Gylam, Jack "Jocco" 115

H

Haberland, Rudolph 64
Hachita 16, 21-22
Hall, John 23
Hall, Thomas. H. 30-31
Hall, Tom 159
Hamilton, Clarence 94
Hamlin, R. C. "Pinky" 90
Hardin, John Wesley 106
Harkey, Dee 39
Harris, W. H. 151
Hart, Edward "Little" 116

203

206

207

Don Bullis is the author of the award-winning series *New Mexico: A Biological Dictionary*, Volumes I and II (Volume III, 2010), and four other non-fiction books on New Mexico history—*New Mexico & Politicians of the Past*, *Old West Trivia Book*, *New Mexico's Finest: Peace Officers Killed in the Line of Duty* (4th Edition, 2010), and *99 New Mexicans ...and a Few Other Folks*. He is also the author of the popular novel, *Bloodville*, and the award-winning *Bull's Eye*. A newspaper columnist for nearly 30 years, his work has also appeared in the *New Mexico Stockman*, *Tradición Revista* and *New Mexico Magazine*. He is a frequent speaker on New Mexico historical subjects.

LaVergne, TN USA
27 November 2010
206496LV00005B/243/P